Secrets of RVing on a Dime and a Dream

Frugal RVing on $1,000 a Month or Less

By Jerry Minchey
www.LifeRV.com

Stony River Media

Minchey, Jerry. Frugal RVing / Jerry Minchey 2018.02

ISBN-13: 978-1-947020-06-1

1. Recreational vehicle living.

Published by Stony River Media

Knoxville, TN

StonyRiverMedia.com

Disclaimer

The information in this book is based on the author's knowledge, experience, and opinions. The methods described in this book are not intended to be a definitive set of instructions. You may discover other methods and materials to accomplish the same end result. Your results may differ.

There are no representations or warranties, express or implied, about the completeness, accuracy or reliability of the information, products, services or related materials contained in this book. The information is provided "as is," to be used at your own risk.

This book is not intended to give legal or financial advice and is sold with the understanding that the author is not engaged in rendering legal, accounting, or other professional services or advice. If legal or financial advice or other expert assistance is required, the services of a competent professional should be sought to ensure you fully understand your obligations and risks.

This book includes information regarding the products and services of third parties. I do not assume responsibility for any third-party materials or opinions. Use of mentioned third party materials does not guarantee your results will mirror those mentioned in the book.

Dedicated to my parents, Charles and Helen Minchey, who taught me to enjoy traveling and enjoy life.

Table of Contents

Introduction 1

Chapter 1: Do You Have the Dream? 11

Chapter 2: RVing is Not All Rainbows, Sunsets, and Margaritas 15

Chapter 3: What Would Life Be Like Living in an RV? 23

Chapter 4: Emotional Aspects of RVing 31

Chapter 5: Is Fear Holding You Back? 39

Chapter 6: Solo RVing 49

Chapter 7: What if I Decide I Don't Like the RVing Lifestyle? 57

Chapter 8: How RVers Save Money on Food, Gas, Camping, and Maintenance 65

Chapter 9: How is it Possible to RV on $1,000 a Month? .. 73

Chapter 10: Learn to RV on $1K a month, Then Find a Way to Make More 87

Chapter 11: How RVers Make Money on the Road 91

Chapter 12: Grow Your Skill Set and Make Even More 99

Chapter 13: How to Buy a Reliable RV at a Great Price... 107

Chapter 14: Domicile, Mail, Healthcare, Internet, Banking, Pets, and Kids 123

Chapter 15: Safety and Security Concerns 149

Chapter 16: Make a Decision 155

Chapter 17: How to Get Rid of Your Stuff 159

Chapter 18: Make it Happen 167

Chapter 19: Summing It All Up 175

Chapter 20: Other Resources 181

Did You Like This Book? 207

Other books by the author available on Amazon 209

Introduction

"You only live once, but if you do it right, once is enough."

~ Mae West

Can you really RV on a dime and a dream? The simple answer is yes you can.

I'm sure you have the dime (if you don't, let me know and I will send you one), but I can't send you the dream. You have to have your own dream.

My guess is that you already have your dream, or you wouldn't be reading this book.

So now that you have your dime and your dream, you have everything you need. But wait—

There are two other things that are keeping a lot of people from living the RVing lifestyle.

The good news is that both of these things are available on Amazon for less than $25 total. I'll tell you what they are in a minute.

A lot of people worry about the uncertainty of living the full-time RVing life. They worry about things such as:

- Will I like the lifestyle?

- Can I afford it?

- What if I don't like the lifestyle?

- Will my friends think I've lost my mind?

- Will I be safe?

- Will I get lonely?

- Will I fail?

- And the list of worries goes on and on.

All you need to answer all of these questions is a crystal ball. You can get one on Amazon. Below is one that's available for $16.90 with free shipping.
Amazon.com/dp/B00E3IYBJG

If you want to save some money

You could save money by using a marble. After all, what's a marble except a little crystal ball? I know what you're thinking. *These are big decisions. I'll need a big crystal ball—not some little one like a marble.*

I agree with you, go ahead and get the big $16 crystal ball, so you will be sure to see all the unknowns.

There is one more thing you will need

A lot of time we have all of the facts and information we need, and we make a decision to do something, but then we never get around to it.

Rather than waiting until you get around to it, just order one from Amazon. There are a lot of "tuits" for sale on Amazon, but make sure you get a round one.

Below are two round tuits that I found on Amazon. Either one of them looks like it will do the job.

I know, it's not a laughing matter, but think about it. Do you really have a reason why you're not enjoying the RVing lifestyle, or will a crystal ball and a round tuit get the decision made and make it happen?

Yes, there are some real reasons why some people can't live the lifestyle right now, but for a lot of people, I think it comes down to not being able to make a decision and then make it happen.

In this book, I will cut out the hype (and there's plenty of hype going around on the internet about living the RVing lifestyle). I will tell it like it is.

To start with, let me say that this lifestyle is not for everyone. I will concentrate on what you need to know to hit the road and show you step-by-step how to do it on a dime and a dream.

In this book I'll be taking you on an educational journey and sharing the knowledge I've learned from my six years of full-time RVing. Hopefully, I'll have you laughing a lot along the way, too.

I have written 10 books about living the RVing lifestyle

Each book deals with a different aspect of the RVing lifestyle, from topics such as RVing on Social Security, RV Retirement, Young RVers, etc. In each of the books, I try to cover the things that are unique to that topic. But, as you might imagine, there are some things (actually, a lot of things) about RVing that are important regardless of the basic aspect of the RVing lifestyle the book is describing.

I'm always faced with a dilemma about what to include in each book. There are important things that someone just getting started in the RVing lifestyle needs to know. Things like how do you read the date code on a tire? How do you get your mail when you're on the road? How do you find free camping places? The list goes on and on.

If I don't cover these basic topics, the person buying the book will be in the dark and could make some big and expensive mistakes when they start out on their RVing adventure.

On the other hand, if I do cover these topics in every book, readers of my books can (and will) say that I'm just repeating some of the information they have already read in one of my other books.

In my previous books, I've kind of split the difference and included some of the really important RVing information in each book. That's what I'll be doing in this book. I won't leave you hanging. But most of the information in this book will be digging into the nitty-gritty topic of *how to live full time in an RV on less than $1,000 a month.* That's basically what the subtitle promised, and that's what you're going to get.

Explaining a few terms

There are a few terms that I will be using throughout this book and I want to explain or define them before we continue.

BLM stands for Bureau of Land Management. BLM land is land that is owned by the government and in most cases is available for free camping. Sometimes there's a 14-day limit. Most BLM land is in the West but not all of it. The government owns 47% of the land in the West, but there are still plenty of places where you can camp for free.

A **toad** is the car that's being towed behind an RV. It's like a dingy for a boat.

When I talk about gas, I'm referring to both gasoline and diesel fuel.

Boondocking refers to camping where there are no hook-ups—no water, electric, or sewer. It's usually free.

Workamping refers to the practice of working 20 or so hours a week in exchange for free camping, and in some cases, you'll also get a small salary. There is even a publication called *Workamper News* that lists thousands of openings for this kind of work. You can find it at this link: **Workamper.com**

Fresh Water Tank holds the fresh water in your RV for use when you don't have hook-ups.

Blackwater is the water from your toilet.

Grey-water is the water from your shower and sinks.

Shore Power is a boating term that RVers use to refer to the electricity you get when you plug your RV into an AC outlet.

One more point: The subtitle of this book is *Frugal RVing on $1,000 a Month or Less.* Even if your budget gives you more than $1,000 a month, you might find that getting your living expenses down close to $1,000 a month and living below your means most of the time will give you more freedom and a lot more joy.

Don't wait for things to get easier, simpler, or better. Life will always be complicated. Learn to be happy right now. Otherwise, you'll run out of time. You will never have all of the answers. Most of the full-time RVers I talk to say their only regret is that they didn't do it sooner.

A few disappointments: I've lived full time in my motorhome now for six years, and overall I have to say it's been a wonderful experience. Although there have been a few heartaches and disappointments—like times when I discovered that my coffee cup was empty.

By the way, if you're impatient or already know a lot about the RVing lifestyle and are 100% convinced that living full time in an RV is what you want to do, and you just want to know how you can do it on $1,000 a month, you can skip the first seven chapters and jump directly to Chapter 8. In Chapter 8 and the following chapters, you will learn how to live the RVing lifestyle on $1,000 a month or less.

One final point: This book was written so that each chapter stands alone. You don't have to read the book straight through from front to back. You can jump around and read the topics that are the most interesting to you first, and then go back and read the other chapters.

Because the chapters are meant to include all of the information about the topic being discussed, you will find that I have included some information in more than one chapter. In other words, you will find some duplication of content in a few places.

There will also be places where I have linked to a video that was linked to in a previous chapter. I do this when I think it's the best video to illustrate the point I'm making. You probably won't stop and watch all of the videos I link to, but if I link to a video two times, by all means, take the time to watch it.

The small amount of duplication and repetition is meant to make the book more useful to you when you're referring back to a chapter. I can see how this could be annoying to you if you're reading the book straight through, but, hopefully, you will find it helpful when you go back to a chapter to go over a topic for a second time.

Bottom line: If you dream of living a life that you don't need a vacation from, keep reading and I'll show you how to do it and, yes, I'll show you how to do it on a dime and a dream. Continue reading and you'll discover that it's your decision which lifestyle you live—your present lifestyle or the RVing lifestyle.

You'll find that it's not a matter of whether you can afford to live in an RV; it's a matter of do you want to?

Let's get started and find out how to **RV on a Dime and a Dream**.

Chapter 1

Do You Have the Dream?

"Happiness is a direction, not a place."

~ Sydney J. Harris

By having a dream, I don't mean a dream such as, "Full-time RVing would be nice," kind of dream. No, I'm not talking about just the ordinary, everyday kind of dream.

I'm talking about an unrealistic, crazy sort of dream that makes your heart sing and brings a little light into the dull routine of your day.

That's the way Becky Schade described the kind of dream you need in her book, *The Little Guide to Dreaming Big*. If you need help formulating your dream, here's a link to Becky's book:

Amazon.com/dp/1545511896

Brittany and Eric at **RvWanderlust.com** put it this way: "We chose the RV lifestyle not to escape life, but so that life doesn't escape us." It's something to think about.

Imagine what it would be like to live and travel full time in your RV—traveling and changing your location anytime you want to.

Hold that picture and thought in your mind and then compare that to your life now. Which way would you be happier? You can't decide until you start dreaming and picturing yourself living the RV lifestyle. In other words...

Nothing will happen until you start dreaming

When we were kids, we were always dreaming and playing make-believe. As we got older, dreaming was frowned upon. Daydreaming was more or less considered to be goofing off.

Forget about the stigma that sometimes goes with dreaming and just start dreaming.

And if your dreams don't scare you, maybe they're not big enough.

A lot of people think of a dream as wishful thinking. For example, they dream of winning the lottery.

But that kind of dream won't cut it. If you're going to make RVing a reality, your dream has to be more than wishful thinking. It has to be a burning desire. It has to be something that you're going to make happen come hell or high water, as the saying goes.

Have a dream, go for it, and make it happen.

Bottom line: Having your dream is the most important thing when it comes to RVing on a dime and a dream. Do you have that dream?

As the words in the song from *South Pacific* say, **"If you don't have a dream, how you gonna have a dream come true?"**

Chapter 2

RVing is Not All Rainbows, Sunsets, and Margaritas

"Life's tragedy is we get old too soon and wise too late."

~ Benjamin Franklin

Since you're reading this book, my guess is you've already been indoctrinated somewhat about how wonderful the RVing lifestyle is.

It's wonderful—at least a lot of people think it is—but that's not the whole story. Let me start with some of the not so fun or glamorous things about the RVing lifestyle that no one has told you about.

Here are some of the things that are not so wonderful about RVing

- If you like to work on things, there is always something on an RV that needs to be fixed. If you don't like to work on things, there is still always something on an RV that needs to be fixed.

- There's no way around it. You can't take all of your "stuff" with you. You have to get rid of a LOT of things. For most people, getting rid of almost all of their stuff is the hardest part about getting ready to hit the road. The good news is that most people find out that they don't miss any of the stuff they got rid of and they are happier without it.

- Face it—there is not a lot of space in an RV. It's a totally different way to live. If there's going to be more than one person traveling, you could get on each other's nerves at times.

- RVs depreciate, and new ones depreciate fast. With a house, you're living in an asset that, hopefully, is going up in value. The opposite is true when you live in an RV. When most people talk about how much it costs them to live in their RV, they leave out the part about how much their RV is decreasing in value each year. If you have an old RV and you're making improvements each year, maybe it's not depreciating much or at all, but the typical RV loses value every year.

- Medical care can be expensive if you're not old enough to be on Medicare. Not being close to your regular doctors can be a big problem if you have many health issues. Also, for most health insurance plans, when you're out of network, medical care gets a lot more expensive. This is discussed in more detail in Chapter 14. (Keep in mind that, like all RVing problems, there are solutions to these problems.)

- For some people, constantly being away from friends and family (especially grandkids) can be a big problem. And for some people it's a deal killer.

- For most people, when they become full-time RVers, they have to learn to get by with less income. If you like to go shopping, buy a lot of new clothes, and always have the latest gadgets, the RVing lifestyle might not be worth the sacrifices required.

So, what's the real story when it comes to RVing?

If you want to know the pros and cons of living the full-time RV lifestyle, you might think that you can just visit an RV park, ask several of the RVers there what they think and get the real scoop.

But that's not the case. Most of the people you find in an RV park love the lifestyle. If they didn't, they wouldn't be there. You will get a one-sided view for sure.

If you watch many YouTube videos about the RVing lifestyle or follow any RVing blogs, you could end up thinking that RVing really is all rainbows, sunsets, and margaritas.

You can experience a lot of all three (with a little effort), but that's not the complete story.

It's kind of like Tom Sawyer describing how much fun it can be whitewashing a fence.

By the way, if you don't know much about whitewashing, allow me to explain.

When I was a little boy (a long, long time ago), my grandmother (and everybody else in the Tennessee hills) would whitewash everything in sight each spring.

Recently, it has become popular to use the term "whitewashing" to mean covering something up. But the original use of the word was to describe a solution of lime and water to make a form of dirt-cheap white paint.

It was water soluble, and most of it would wash away in a few months, but it was a common practice every spring to use the solution to paint everything white—and I do mean everything.

Every spring my grandmother wanted the fence around the yard, the tree trunks in the yard, and even big rocks in the yard to all be whitewashed.

As a kid, whitewashing things every year was a lot of fun to start with, but, like Tom Sawyer, the new soon wore off and it became work. I wasn't as smart as ole Tom and I had to keep whitewashing things until everything in sight was white.

Whitewashing things in the spring was as routine as buttercups blooming. It meant that spring had arrived. Anyone who didn't whitewash everything around their house and yard, basically just didn't give a damn. At least, that was the general thinking in the Tennessee hills back in the 1950s—just like it was in Hannibal, Missouri back in the 1800s when Tom Sawyer was a boy.

I'm sure that's more than you wanted to know about whitewashing, and you might be thinking, what does this have to do with *RVing?*

It's just a simple story to demonstrate that perception and reality depend a lot on how a situation is described. That's the case when it comes to describing the RVing lifestyle for sure.

People who like the lifestyle can (and do) make it sound like Heaven on Earth. People who hate it make it sound like being one step above (or maybe one step below) sleeping on the street.

The good parts of the RVing lifestyle

I could say it's all good. I don't remember any bad experiences. There have been times when things have broken or stopped working, but that's just part of the adventure. If there were no unknowns or problems, there would be no adventure.

So, yes, there are many good parts of the RVing lifestyle. I'm sure you already have several ideas about why you want to live in an RV.

You can learn about a lot more enjoyable things RVers like by watching some of the thousands of YouTube videos that other RVers have posted. Check out some of my favorite videos listed in Chapter 20, Other Resources.

One of the things I like best about RVing is the freedom to go anywhere, anytime I want to. I also love the people I meet, and I love the adventurous spirit they have. I like to see what's around the next curve or over the next hill. I know that sounds like a cliché, but it's how I feel. I truly love the RVing lifestyle. If I didn't, I wouldn't still be RVing going on seven years—with no plans to change.

Continue reading this book and by the time you finish it, I think you will know enough to decide if RVing is the right lifestyle for you.

One thing to keep in mind is that one of the best things about choosing the RVing lifestyle is that if you decide it's not right for you, it's easy to sell your RV (and maybe even make a profit on it as I'll explain later in Chapter 13), and then move on to a different lifestyle, such as living on a boat, living in a different country, living on a farm or whatever you think would be the best lifestyle for you.

One thing is for sure—whatever you decide, my guess is that you will not want to go back to the lifestyle you're living now. You're ready for a change.

Bottom line: It's true that the RVing lifestyle is not all rainbows, sunsets, and margaritas, but enough of it is that, after living full time in my RV for six years, I wouldn't want to go back to living in a stick and brick house, condo or apartment. No way. (And I don't even like margaritas.)

Chapter 3

What Would Life Be Like Living in an RV?

"If you want a happy ending, that depends, of course, on where you stop your story."

~ Orson Welles

If you're wondering what life would be like living in an RV, I could sum it up by saying, "It will be wonderful," but you probably want to know more about it than that. So, let's dig a little deeper.

One thing is for sure. It won't be boring, and it won't be mundane or routine.

Videos that describe the RVing life

Below are links to some short videos that do a great job of showing what life is like living full time in an RV. Whether you're a retired couple, you're young and raising a family, or you plan to RV solo, I think you will be able to picture yourself in one of these videos.

Note: I've found that for most videos I can select the speed as 1.5x instead of "Normal" and still understand what's being said. This technique allows me to watch the videos in less time. Of course, they're more enjoyable when you watch them at the normal speed.

Two videos you really should watch

These first two videos are ones that I think you really should watch to get a good idea of what the RVing life is all about. The other four are good too, but by all means take the time to watch the first two.

Vimeo.com/71385845 — This must-watch 7-minute video shows a young couple traveling with their small son. Even if you're not a young couple that will be traveling with a small child, I still think this is a video you should watch.

YouTube.com/watch?v=ebbo800_Rg0 — Becky Schade is a single female in her 30s. She has been living full time as a solo-RVer for 6 years now in her tiny camper. If you're wondering how she likes living full time in such a small

RV, she is selling the small RV she has and has bought an even smaller one. She loves living small. With a smaller RV, she can go to a lot more boondocking places.

These next six videos provide even more examples of what it would be like living full time in an RV

YouTube.com/watch?v=2oE5EQ9SSFE — This is an interview with a retired couple talking about their life as full-time RVers.

YouTube.com/watch?v=E6_AYrdfDS0 — In this video Nathan and Marissa tell it like it is. They talk about what they wish they had known before they started living the RVing lifestyle. They also talk about how things change. They have had four totally different RVs during their first two years of RVing.

YouTube.com/watch?v=X1EIdQN5rq0 — Pippi Peterson is a single female who lives full time in her Class A motorhome. She does most of her own maintenance and enjoys the freedom of her lifestyle.

YouTube.com/watch?v=bkiK5ZUgLT8 — Here is a link to a 39-second video made three years later in Pippi's life. As a further update, since this video was posted she has sold her 1992 Class A motorhome and now has a fifth-wheel camper and truck. (Note that RVers often change their minds about which type of RV is best for their lifestyle.)

Youtube.com/watch?v=JszEEQg1cao — Rachel and James RVing in a van.

Youtube.com/watch?v=BsEs-CLBbaU&t-98s – Marc and Tricia travel with their three kids and have posted several fun, interesting, and informative RVing videos.

As you can see from this sample of videos about the different ways people live in their RVs, there's no one way to describe what it is like to live full time in an RV, but hopefully these videos will give you some ideas about what your life would be like living the RVing lifestyle.

Did you see yourself in any of these videos? Did they help you formulate your dream?

Remember, having your dream is the most important thing when it comes to RVing on a dime and a dream.

In Chapter 20, Other Resources, I provide links to a lot of other videos I like and recommend. The videos I've listed here give you a representative sample of life as a full-time RVer. Take the time to watch them, and you will have a much better idea of what it will be like to live full time in an RV.

You'll find that age doesn't matter to RVers

In a normal society, people tend to hang out together in groups based on their age. After all, young people are not interested in the same things that older people are—and vice versa.

That's not the case when you're RVing. Young and old alike have a common interest—RVing.

Regardless of your age, you will be part of the tribe. When you're sitting around the campfire telling tales, asking questions, and just generally having a good time, you'll find that it's all just one big tribe.

RVers are in control of their lives

One of the best parts about the RVing lifestyle is that you are in complete control. You can make it whatever you want it to be. You can go where you want to go, stay as long as you want, and then move on to somewhere else.

Some people like to do a lot of traveling and move on every few days. I like to stay in one place for at least two weeks and, for me, staying for a month or longer is even better.

I like to spend time in the summer in the cool North Carolina mountains, and I like to move higher up in the mountains as the summer starts getting warmer. I like to spend the winters in Florida. In other words, I try to stay where the temperature is comfortable, and I spend most of my time in the eastern part of the US.

Most RVers I know like the western part of the US better for RVing. You have southern Arizona, New Mexico, and parts of Texas for the winter months and the cooler northwest coast and the Rockies for the summer months.

Another advantage of RVing in the western part of the US is that there is a lot of what's called BLM (Bureau of Land Management) land. You can camp on most of the BLM land totally free. Sometimes there are rules, such as you can only stay in one place for 14 days, etc., but it's a great way to camp without paying campground fees. I'll talk more about that later in the book.

There are some low-cost camping options in the eastern part of the US, but you have to look a little harder for them.

I just spent 14 days boondocking in the Pisgah National Forest in North Carolina. It wasn't free, but at $2.50 a night, it's pretty close. You can only camp there for 14 days before having to leave for 30 days. It's normally $5.00 a night, but I got the $2.50 rate because I had the America the Beautiful Senior Pass.

This is one of my favorite places in the mountains to boondock. I usually camp there a few weeks every year.

Bottom line: Life in an RV can and will be anything you want it to be. You can live where you want to, stay as long as you want, and move when you want. You'll have more freedom than you've ever had in your life, and you will even have the freedom to stop living the RVing life and live a totally different life any time you want to. What a wonderful way to live—at least that's the way I see it.

Chapter 4

Emotional Aspects of RVing

"All emotion is involuntary when genuine."

~ Mark Twain

As Mark Twain said, we don't have any control over the emotions we feel. They are involuntary.

We do, however, have some control over how we deal with our emotions, and that's what this chapter is about.

Since this book is about how to RV on a dime and a dream, my guess is that you have probably more or less already made up your mind that you want to live the RVing lifestyle, but you still have a few nagging concerns from time to time as you think more about the process.

You may be thinking: Will it really work for me and will I be happy? When you're making this big of a change in your life, there will be a lot of emotions to deal with.

Yes, one big factor to consider when deciding whether to live the RVing lifestyle is the emotional aspect.

One of the biggest emotions you'll have to deal with is the constant gnawing feeling of "What if."

You can analyze all the numbers and the financial part of RVing, but you can't put a number on the emotional part. This is the biggest unknown and probably the scariest part of setting out on living the RVing lifestyle.

Here are some of the major emotional concerns

- Will my family and friends think I've lost my mind? (Some may think you're crazy—others will be sure.)

- Will I get lonely?

- Am I being realistic?

- Will I run out of money?

- Is this a mistake?

- What if my RV breaks down and leaves me stranded?

- What if I get sick?

- Will living 24/7 in a cramped space with my spouse and family drive me crazy?

- If I'm RVing solo, how will I handle living 24/7 by myself—especially if I'm boondocking and not around other people?

- Can I deal with being away from family and friends?

RVing emotions fall into one of two categories

The emotions you will have to deal with as an RVer will fall into one of two broad categories—emotions before you hit the road and emotions after you get on the road.

Emotions you'll have to deal with before you get on the road

Here are some of the emotions you will be dealing with before you hit the road:

- Selling your house or moving out of your apartment

- Getting rid of your stuff

- Dealing with reactions and comments from family and friends

- Going over and over the numbers and deciding if you can really do it

- Dealing with all the unknowns

- The constant "what if" questions in your head

Maybe keeping the following quotes in mind will help you deal with the unknowns of your RVing adventure.

"Life is either a great adventure or nothing at all."

~ Helen Keller

"Whenever you find yourself on the side of the majority, it's time to pause and reflect."

~ Mark Twain

Emotions you'll experience after you get on the road

- Being away from family and friends

- Unexpected problems and expenses

- Will my money run out?

- Do I have enough money in my emergency fund?

- Did I buy the right RV?

- What if my sources of income dry up?

Feelings to expect after you hit the road

You'll be questioning yourself for a while after you hit the road. This questioning is normal. The future is unknown, but, realistically, it's unknown in your present lifestyle too.

Accept the fact that the emotions and doubts you feel when you first start out are normal. They will fade quickly when the excitement kicks in. How can you feel down when every day is a new adventure?

Face the fact that there will be a huge emotional challenge when you leave your home, job, family, and friends all at once. This can be a big blow. It can even be downright scary. Accept that this feeling is normal.

Problems will arise

Nathan and Marissa (check out their YouTube channel at *Less Junk, More Journey*) planned for over a year: selling their house, deciding on the right RV for their needs, and getting ready to embark on their full-time RVing journey. They had everything planned to the nth degree.

Then they hit the road and their RV broke down less than 30 minutes after they pulled out. They had to get their RV towed and delay the start of their RVing adventure until the repairs could be made.

My guess is that your luck will be better than theirs, and you will live happily ever after—or at least for more than 30 minutes before you start running into problems.

One important thing to keep in mind

If you're going to be RVing with someone else, it's important to make sure both parties really want to live the RVing lifestyle.

I've seen it time and time again. One person is gung-ho, and the other person reluctantly goes along with the idea. It can work and sometimes it does.

I've even seen cases where the reluctant person ends up liking the plan more than the one who originally proposed the idea, but that's not normally the case.

I was talking to a woman last week. She and her husband had been living full time in their 44-foot Class A motorhome for about six months. Her husband had to buy the large 44-foot motorhome before she would even consider living in an RV.

They were from Virginia and were planning on going to Colorado for three months when the "check engine light" came on. It turned out to be a minor thing. I think it was a defective oxygen sensor.

Anyway, she said, "That's it. We have to get rid of this thing and go back to living in a house. What if we got to Colorado and that happened?" Their motorhome was only about four years old and in good condition.

Maybe someone should have told her that they have RV repair shops in Colorado.

They should have seriously discussed the idea before they sold their house and bought a motorhome. And the important thing is that they both should have listened to what the other person was saying and paid attention to what each of them really wanted to do. I'm sure they discussed it, but my guess is that they each heard what they wanted to hear.

Living in an RV won't fix all the problems in your life.

If you have emotional baggage, getting out of Dodge won't make it go away.

You will have a lot of emotions to deal with both before and after you hit the road. Look at your emotions as a good thing. They force you to consider all the "what if" thoughts that come to mind. These need to be considered—and maybe more than once, but at some point, you have to decide that you've considered everything and are prepared to deal with events if and when they happen.

Bottom line: If there were no unknowns, there wouldn't be any adventure. So, embrace the idea that unexpected good

things and unexpected bad things are going to happen.
Enjoy the adventure.

One more important point: I've talked about several
emotions in this chapter, but I haven't talked about the
elephant in the room—the emotion of fear.

I didn't leave fear out because it wasn't important but
because it's so important that I've devoted the whole next
chapter to it.

Chapter 5

Is Fear Holding You Back?

"Don't let the noise of others' opinions drown out your own inner voice. And most important, have the courage to follow your heart and intuition."

~ Steve Jobs

If you have a dream of living full time in an RV and you're not doing it yet, my guess is that fear is holding you back. It's not the money (although maybe it's the fear of running out of money).

The idea of taking a risk conjures up feelings of fear. It's a normal and natural reaction. Fear helps keep us safe, but sometimes it's easy to let fear have more control over our actions than is warranted.

One of the best ways to overcome fear is to arm yourself with knowledge and information. The more you know about a situation, the less fear there will be in the decision to go forward.

I think that's what you're doing by reading this book. You're getting the information you need to make an informed decision and to implement it.

Another way to overcome fear is to do whatever it is you're afraid of. I remember the first time I was driving my 34-foot Class A motorhome all the way across Atlanta and I was towing a car with the front wheels on a dolly.

About the time I was ready to breathe a sigh of relief because I was almost through Atlanta, I made a wrong turn and ended up back downtown, and I had to do it all over again. It was scary, but I made it.

An even worse driving experience for me was driving my motorhome with my car in tow through the narrow streets of downtown St. Augustine, Florida. I think those streets were just barely wide enough for a horse and buggy. But, again, I made it.

After you've done something once, it doesn't seem as scary. That's why I say doing something is a good way to overcome the fear of doing it.

Fear shows up in many forms

The fear of getting hurt—like why we didn't want to jump off of the high diving board when we were kids—is not the fear you're dealing with here. You don't really think you might get hurt if you start living the RVing lifestyle.

Here are some of the fears you're probably concerned about (even though you may not want to admit all of them).

- Fear that your friends will think you're being totally irresponsible

- Fear that you'll run out of money

- Fear that you'll blow what money you have and have to come home and try to find a job and a place to live

- Fear that you won't like the lifestyle and then have to admit that you were wrong

- Fear of embarrassment when things don't work out

- Fear of being assaulted when you're RVing by yourself

My guess is that your biggest fear is that you won't be able to earn the money it will take to make it work, that it won't work out, and then you'll have to listen to your family and friends saying, "I told you so." Even if they don't say it, you know they will be thinking it.

Most people don't want to admit it, but these are the fears that keep a lot of people from taking the plunge and living full time in an RV.

Keep reading, and I'll show you how you can be convinced that you really can make it work and how you can live in your RV on a dime and a dream. After all, that's what the title of the book promised, so keep reading and let me prove to you that you can do it.

Something to think about

There's an old saying meant to remind you that you don't have to get involved with other people's drama.

The saying is, "It's not my circus and not my monkeys." Sometimes it's good to keep that saying in mind.

But what if you look at your life and realize that this is your circus and those are your monkeys?

In other words, this is your life, and it's going to continue just as it is unless you make some changes.

Does this describe your present life?

The alarm clock goes off, and you start your morning in a rushed mode (because you didn't want to get up any earlier than absolutely necessary). You get ready for work as fast as possible, gobble down some excuse for breakfast, and grab a cup of coffee to take with you as you head out the door for your commute to work.

You watch the clock all day, wanting to go home, and then the next morning it's lather, rinse, repeat.

This routine might be somewhat okay if you were getting ahead, but are you any better off now than you were this time last year? How much more went into savings over the past year?

Making a change involves taking a risk

A lot of people land a decent job and ride it until they retire. That's the safe way to live life. That may be what you've been doing so far, but is that what you want to do for the rest of your life, or do you want to take a risk and do something totally different?

How many people do you know who thought their job was secure until they went to work one day and found out that it wasn't? It's something to think about. In other words, how much security do you really have?

Whether you're 27, 72, or somewhere in between, you can start now and live a totally different life.

Maybe you don't want a totally different life; you only want a slightly different life. For example, you want to keep your dog (and maybe your spouse), but you would like to see almost everything else change.

Up until the last few years, quitting your job and living full time in an RV was not a realistic option for most people, but now technology (and a lot of other things) has changed all of that.

That's one of the reasons more than 1,000 new RVs a day are being sold.

It's no longer a matter of whether you can afford to quit your job and live full time in an RV. The only question is, "Do you really want to?"

Later in this book, I'll convince you that you can afford to do it, but, for now, take my word for it.

RV living can be inexpensive

Living in an RV can be inexpensive because campsites can be free and power (with the use of solar) can also be free. Basically, you'll need to pay for food, insurance, a few personal items, and that's it. That's the bare minimum, but you'll probably want to spend a little more.

I'll get into all of that later in the book.

I don't mean you have to sit at your desk and work on your computer (although that's one option).

Employers now recognize RVers as being hard-working, dependable employees. They're eager to hire them. For example, Amazon hires thousands of RVers, paying them a good salary and providing them with a free place to camp in order to have them work during October, November, and December to help meet the Christmas demand.

Almost all campgrounds (along with state and federal parks) hire RVers to work a few hours a week in exchange for free camping and usually a small salary.

Lots of other income producing opportunities for RVers will be described later in the book.

The risk of change

I have lived full time in my motorhome for six years now. Before that, I lived in Costa Rica for six months.

There are so many interesting lifestyles out there to choose from. You don't have to stick with just one—I didn't. In fact, I've already made arrangements to go back to Costa Rica to live for a few months in the spring of 2019. (Not in my motorhome, of course.)

Most people think they're locked into the way they're living now.

Society and advertising have brainwashed most of us into believing that we need to keep working, accumulating more and more stuff, take a two-week vacation every year (when we can afford it), and be happy.

Most people have a reasonably new car or two (with payments), and they think they've achieved the American Dream.

I think you've about decided that there must be more to life than this and that's why you're reading this book.

You want to know if you have options, and, if so, how you can turn them into reality.

As you read this book, you will see that there's a whole new world waiting for you out there. You'll learn what it's like to live full time in an RV. You'll also learn how you can afford to live this lifestyle while putting more money in savings every year than you're doing now.

One final thought: You can't plan everything regardless of how much time you take getting everything ready for your RVing adventure. When I was in engineering school, almost all of my time was spent learning how to design things. But when I started working as an engineer, I found out that I spent a lot more time testing designs than I ever spent doing the actual designs. I found out that's the way engineering works. In school, I don't remember ever testing anything.

You've planned everything. Your testing will start when you hit the road.

You can't plan for everything. Well, actually, you can. It's called an emergency fund.

There may be valid reasons why you can't live full time in an RV right now (aging parents you need to take care of, a business or house you need to sell, etc.), but don't let fear be one of them. Fear is useful to help you make sure you've looked at all of the factors involved, but it shouldn't be a reason not to take the plunge.

Bottom line: Don't be afraid that something will go wrong. Accept the fact that for sure something will go wrong, and then something else will go wrong. That's the RVing lifestyle. If you can't handle that, this life is not for you.

Fear will never go away completely, but as you gain confidence in your ability to handle the different situations that full-time RV living throws at you, fear will lose its control over you. Fear is useful to make sure you do your research and consider the risks, but it should not have veto power over your decisions.

Chapter 6

Solo RVing

"The man who goes alone can start today; but he who travels with another must wait till that other is ready."

~ Henry David Thoreau

Yep, ole Henry hit the nail on the head with that statement. Maybe he was talking about RVing when he said that, but probably not since he died in 1862. But who knows, he was a forward thinker.

There are a lot of advantages to RVing solo. I have been RVing solo for over six years. I don't even have a dog. It's just me and my motorhome. I love the lifestyle, and I like the idea of traveling alone. I don't have any plans to change.

The decisions are mine to make, and the consequences are mine to bear.

Don't worry RVing solo

If you're concerned about traveling solo, my simple answer is don't be. I meet a lot, and I do mean a lot, of solo RVers. (Surprisingly, I see more women solo RVers than men.)

Contrary to what I expected, I've never met a solo RVer who has ever experienced any loneliness or security concerns while traveling as a solo RVer.

Tom Petty pretty well summed it up in his quote shown below:

"Most things I worry about never happen anyway."

~ Tom Petty

It's easy to say, "Don't worry," but I'm sure you would like to have some information and facts to keep you from worrying. Let me fill in some blanks.

There's no riff-raff in RV parks

One of the main reasons RVing is safe is that there is no riff-raff in RV campgrounds or in the boondocking places RVers go.

Think about it, if a person wanted to steal something, the pickings are not very good inside of an RV. What would they steal? There's nothing in an RV that someone could walk off with and sell except maybe a computer. Take an old computer into a pawn shop and see what they will offer you for it.

I don't think I have locked my motorhome in over a year. (Maybe I should start now since I've told the world that my motorhome is sitting there unlocked.)

Even if someone tried to break into your RV, blowing your horn (or opening the window and screaming) would quickly bring more help and bring it faster than if you called 911 while living in a traditional house or apartment.

In other words, with a little common sense and reasonable precautions, you're safer in an RV than you would be in most houses or apartments.

11 things to consider when traveling solo

- **Arrive at your campground well before dark.** Don't push it close because traffic and other factors can make your trip take longer than expected. It's hard to judge the safety of a camping place after dark, and it's a lot easier to get backed in and set up when it's daylight. Also, it's a good idea to meet your neighbors before dark.

- **Meet your neighbors and let them know that you are traveling solo.** (This is particularly important for women traveling solo.) This is contrary to what a lot of people suggest. Some go so far as to tell women traveling solo to set a pair of large men's boots outside the door of their RV, and when they leave their RV, they should say goodbye to their imaginary traveling companion. I say that this is BS. If you're staying anywhere more than one or two nights, people in the campground are going to know that there is no one else in the RV. Also, your neighbors are a lot more inclined to come to your rescue when you blow your horn if they know you're traveling by yourself.

- **Carry Mace, pepper spray, a gun or whatever you feel comfortable with.** You'll probably never need or use any of these items, but they buy you peace of mind.

- **Have an extra set of keys in a metal magnetic key box hidden in a secure and out-of-the-way place outside**

your RV. Nothing makes you feel more helpless than being locked out of your RV.

- **Have an extra credit card and a few hundred dollars of cash hidden inside your RV.** There are plenty of places in an RV where you can hide things that couldn't be found if someone had all day to look for them. This could really come in handy if you lose your wallet.

- **Have photocopies of the front and back of your driver's license and all of your credit cards, insurance cards, etc.** Keep a copy in your RV, and also leave a copy with a friend or family member.

- **Have a GPS and know how to use it.** Also have a good set of maps.

- **Keep your cell phone with you and keep the battery charged.** You may want to keep an extra battery, particularly if your battery is getting old and doesn't hold a charge for very long. If you spend much time in areas where you don't have a good cell phone signal, consider getting a cell phone booster. Also, have one of the little 12-volt to USB adapters so you can charge your phone from your RV or vehicle.

- **Stay in one location for a week or a month or longer.** When you first arrive at a place, that's when you feel the most insecure. That's because everything is unknown to you. That's natural. The longer you stay in a place the more comfortable you will feel there. It's simple. If you stay in each place for a month at a time, you will spend most of your time feeling comfortable. If you're moving every two or three days, you will spend most of your time feeling a little uncomfortable or apprehensive. Also, you will save money by taking advantage of the lower weekly or monthly rates, you'll cut your gas expense, and you'll have time to explore the area.

- **Keep your RV well maintained.** You don't want breakdowns while you're on the road. Replace belts and hoses as soon as they start showing signs of aging. Also, be sure to check the air pressure in your tires regularly. I have an automatic system that gives me a readout on the dash of the pressure and temperature of each of my six motorhome tires, plus the two dolly tires and the two back tires of my car. In addition to the digital readout, it also sounds an alarm if the pressure of any tire gets outside the safe range I've set. This gives me peace of mind. I consider this to be the best investment I've made when it comes to gadgets or upgrades to my RV.

- **The most important thing to keep in mind is to follow your instincts about safety.** If you pull into a place and your gut tells you that something doesn't seem right, your house has wheels. You can leave.

Most of the above comments are good advice for any RVer—solo or not. There will always be unknowns and things to deal with, but that's part of the adventure of the RVing lifestyle.

By the way, reading the above 11 comments might make you think there are a lot of things that could happen when you're traveling solo. These are all simply precautions to take (mainly to give you peace of mind). I've never known a single time when any of these precautions were actually necessary—well, I did lock myself out of my RV one time.

Solo RVing videos

One way to quickly get a feel for how solo RVers feel about their lifestyle is to watch a few short videos of them talking about their life and experiences.

There are hundreds of solo RVer videos on YouTube. Below are four of my favorites:

Pippi Peterson: Youtube.com/watch?v=X1EIdQN5rq0

Becky Schade:
Youtube.com/watch?v=ebbo800_Rg0&t=2s

Alex: Youtube.com/watch?v=3nMBNAlHQMo&t=7s

Carolyn Rose: Youtube.com/watch?v=xoy3vNUjLOU&t=3s
Luis:

Youtube.com/channel/UCBMYjw2IrXOTZq3q0LUZfqQ

Loneliness is non-existent in the RV world

RVers are a friendly bunch, and you will be welcomed into the tribe whether you're camping in an RV park or with a few RVers out in the boondocks.

So, don't let the fact that you will be traveling solo be a reason not to enjoy the RV lifestyle.

If you think about it, when someone is by themselves in an RV all day talking to the same person, you can be sure they will welcome somebody new to talk to. Maybe that's why RVers are so friendly.

When you realize that loneliness and security are not a problem for solo RVers, what else is there to worry about?

Bottom line: I'm convinced that solo RVers are safer traveling and living in their rigs than they are in their conventional homes. And I know they're having more fun. So, as Mark Twain said, "Throw off the bowlines. Sail away from the safe harbor. Catch the trade winds in your sails. Explore. Dream. Discover."

Chapter 7

What if I Decide I Don't Like the RVing Lifestyle?

"It's tough to make predictions, especially about the future."

~ Yogi Berra

We all want to know what the future holds for us, but we have to accept that what Yogi said in the quote at the beginning of the chapter is true.

Since you're seriously considering living the RVing lifestyle (and I know you are or you wouldn't be reading this book), my guess is that you will like the lifestyle.

But there's still the question of "What if I don't like it?" That's really not as big of a problem as most people first think. The reason is, you're ready for a change in your life. You don't want to continue living your life the way you're living it now.

The RVing lifestyle may not be how you end up living. You may later decide that you want to live on a boat, on a farm, in the mountains, in a condo downtown, or even in a different country. But one thing is for sure, you want to live a different lifestyle.

If you try the RVing lifestyle and decide you don't like it, you're well on your way to your next adventure. You will have gotten rid of most of your stuff and your house or apartment.

Having that out of the way makes moving on to the next phase of your life a lot easier. In other words, you've done the hard part, and now you're free to move on to your next adventure.

You can make money and not lose money by trying the RVing lifestyle

One of the concerns a lot of people have when they're considering the RVing lifestyle is that they're afraid that, if they don't like it, they will end up losing a lot of money.

The good news is you can try RVing, and if you decide you don't like it, you can end up financially better off. Here's how:

The biggest risk is buying an RV and then losing money on it when you decide to sell it. And, yes, you can lose a lot of money on an RV if you buy a new one and then sell it in a year or so. The key to making money is to do your research and buy a used RV for well under the market value. Then you can sell it in a year or so and make a profit on it.

As my father always told me, "You make your money when you buy something—not when you sell it."

Just because you buy used doesn't mean you will get a good deal. You might get a fair price when you buy a used RV from a reputable dealer, but that's not what you want. You want something better than a fair price. You want a bargain price.

By a bargain price, I don't necessarily mean a dirt-cheap price. If you buy an RV at a low price and then find out it has a lot of things wrong with it, that's not a bargain.

Here is a book I think everyone who is even remotely thinking of buying an RV should own:

Buying a Used Motorhome – How to get the most for your money and not get burned (updated March 2017) by Bill Myers

You can get the eBook version from Amazon for $3.99 at the link below:

Amazon.com/dp/B007OV4TBY

Even though this book is mainly about buying a motorhome, a lot of the information in the book will apply to fifth-wheel RVs and campers too.

Don't consider buying an RV (or even looking at one) before you invest $3.99 and buy this book.

Even if you decide you love the RVing lifestyle, there's a good chance that, after a year, you will want a different RV. Over half of the people who have been on the road for two years or more have a different RV than the one they started with.

One of the main reasons new RVers want a different RV after a year or so of being on the road is that they didn't know what kind of RVing life they would be living, and even if they thought they did know, there's a good chance that what they want to do will change.

Surprisingly, after a year or so, most of RVers have a smaller RV than the one they started with. I have one friend who had four RVs in two years. The good part is that he made a profit every time he sold the RV he had.

As I said before, you will probably sell your RV for about what it's worth. Your goal is to buy it for less than it's worth.

If you make some improvements (even just cleaning it up) it helps you make your profit.

Yes, unlike a house, RVs will depreciate in value (new ones will depreciate a lot in the first few years). But if you buy a used one, it will not depreciate much in a year (especially if it's a very used one), and if you bought it at a great price, you can make a profit even after allowing for the depreciation.

In addition to the profit you might make on your RV, you will also save money because your living cost will be less, so yes, your RVing experience could allow you to be financially better off.

One of the good things about living for a year in an RV is that you can do it without spending much money.

The RVing lifestyle can be experienced in several ways

One of the reasons I think you'll like living in an RV is because there are so many ways to live the RVing lifestyle.

- There's the conventional RVing lifestyle of traveling around the country, visiting national parks, staying in campgrounds, basically doing a lot of traveling and seeing the country that most people picture when they think of living in an RV.

- You can stay in one place, and it's kind of like living in a subdivision.

- You can stay in one place in the summer and somewhere warm in the winter.

- You can live off-grid out in nature (this is called boondocking).

- You can travel every day or once a month.

- You don't have to stick with one type of RVing. A lot of RVers live one way for a while and then live a totally different lifestyle for a while.

- And best of all, you can alternate between these ways of RVing. You don't have to live one way all the time.

Of course, there's always the possibility if you're traveling with someone that one of you will like the lifestyle and the other won't. And when you spend 24/7 with someone in a 200-sq. ft. space, you may find out that you're not really that compatible.

I think Mark Twain described that situation pretty well in the quote below:

"I have found that there ain't no surer way to find out whether you like people or hate them than to travel with them."

~ Mark Twain

Bottom line: Since you're thinking about living full time in an RV, you're ready for a change. Go for it. Get rid of your house and most of your junk (I mean valuable stuff) and go for it. If you decide you don't like the RVing lifestyle, then you're free to try another lifestyle—living on a boat, living on a farm, living near the ocean, or living in a different country. The main thing is to make a decision and go for it.

Chapter 8

How RVers Save Money on Food, Gas, Camping, and Maintenance

"Blessed are the cracked, for they shall let in the light."

~ Groucho Marx

If you like to go shopping, buy new clothes, buy the latest gadgets, go to concerts and sporting events, like new cars, want the latest cell phone, and like to eat out all the time, you're going to end up spending as much (and maybe even more) money living in an RV as you're spending now because. . .

Moving into an RV won't change who you are.

You have to make a conscious effort to change your ways. One of the first things you have to do to RV on a dime and a dream is to find ways to live and not spend so many dimes.

How RVers save money

Your best option to save money is to make changes to areas where most of your money is being spent. You can't save any money by cutting back on how much you spend on salt because if you totally eliminated salt, it wouldn't save enough to matter.

I know, I'm being facetious, but I'm doing it to make a point. It reminds me of the mother who said to her kid, "If I've told you once, I've told you a million times. Don't exaggerate."

I got off track. Let's get back to how RVers save money.

To save money, you have to cut back in the areas where you're spending a lot of money. Keep detailed records of every penny you spend for a month or so and you might be surprised at the areas where you're spending money. Armed with this information, you can make some informed decisions about where and how to cut back on your spending.

When you're RVing, here are the areas you need to look at closely

- **Eating out:** First, don't eat out very often. Make it a special occasion. If you eat out a lot, then it's no longer a special occasion. Also, skip the chain restaurants and the tourist places. Eat at the local mom and pop places and you will get to experience the real cuisine of the area.

- **Don't waste food:** Even if you eat most of your meals at home, you may still be wasting a lot of money by throwing away too much food. One way to save a lot on food is to start planning every meal by looking in the refrigerator and seeing what leftovers you have and then thinking what you would need to add to those leftovers to make a good meal. We're all guilty of leaving leftovers in the back of the refrigerator too long and then throwing them out. And we all know ways to save when buying food. We just don't do it. Cut out junk food, shop at discount stores like Aldi, and buy mostly real food—beans, rice, veggies—cut back on protein and high-priced cuts of meat. Also, watch fruits and veggies closely and be sure to eat them before they go bad.

- **Gas (or diesel fuel):** The best way to save money on gas is not to travel as much. Stay in one place for a month or more and enjoy getting to know the area. Also, you can save on gas by going slower. I've found that I get a lot better gas mileage driving at 55 mph than I do at 65. And if I bump it up to 70, my mileage really goes down.

- **Campground fees:** You can save a lot on campground fees by a doing a lot of boondocking (which means camping for free on public land). Some RVers do this almost exclusively. You can also save a lot by staying at campgrounds for a month or more at a time. The monthly rate at most campgrounds is about twice the weekly rate. Many campgrounds have workcamper programs where you can work about 20 hours a week and camp for free. You can join PassPortAmerica.com and camp at over 2,000 campgrounds for half price. There are some restrictions, like in most campgrounds you can only stay for one to three nights and sometimes you can't stay on weekends, but these restrictions are sometimes negotiable. Also, when you're on the road and want to stop for the night, don't pay top dollar to stay at a campground for one night. Stay at a Walmart for free. I do it all the time.

- **RV maintenance:** The Camping World service center near where I'm camping recently raised their hourly rate from $129 an hour to $142 an hour. I use them for some things, but you can save a lot by doing as much of your RV maintenance work yourself as possible. You can learn how to fix a lot of problems by watching YouTube videos. Just describe your problem and you might be amazed at how many videos show up. And, of course, do a lot of preventive maintenance work on your RV. Another way I handle maintenance work is by using a mobile RV tech. He is less expensive, and I get to watch how he fixes something. That way, the next time (and there will be a next time) I can fix it myself. I have also found a reliable truck repair place that charges about 1/3 of what the RV shops charge. The owner of the shop used to have a Class A RV and knows how to repair most things on an RV.

If you could get these five categories down to zero, the RVing lifestyle won't be expensive at all. Of course, you can't get them down to zero, but for most people, these expenses can be cut way down and without any decrease in quality of life or enjoyment—just follow the advice I've outlined.

One other point—don't be a tourist. One of the best ways RVers have found to save money is to stop being a tourist. Many new RVers spend a lot of money when they first start RVing because they act like they're on vacation and do things as though they are a tourist, eating out a lot, spending money on tourist attractions, and just generally acting like they're on vacation.

Remember that you're not on a full-time vacation and you're not a tourist. If you do all of the tourist things, you're going to blow your budget in a hurry. I've had several RVers tell me that they spent a lot more money the first year they were on the road than they do now. They say that it's more fun to be a temporary resident in an area than it is to be a tourist, and, of course, a lot less expensive.

Save and splurge

One advantage of saving a lot of money is that it gives you more money to spend on things that really make you happy. You can do a few tourist things, and buy a few gadgets, but only a few.

I don't spend much on clothes and I don't eat out a lot. (I do like to go out and have a glass of wine and listen to live music from time to time.) Another area where I have to watch my budget is that I like gadgets, especially things for the motorhome.

Here are some of the gadgets I've spent money on over the last year: a five-stage battery charger, two more 6-volt coach batteries, a battery monitoring system, external sensors for the holding tanks so I can get accurate readings of the levels, a new ham radio antenna, a quadcopter to hopefully make my YouTube videos more interesting, and the list goes on.

None of these items were things I had to have. They were just things I wanted. I think you can see how buying gadgets could get out of hand and blow a budget. I have to watch myself (and my budget) because I love gadgets.

There is a group on Facebook called RV Camping on $1,000 a month or less. They have a little over 4,500 members. You can find it at the link below:

Facebook.com/groups/1659780414258697

Bottom line: Follow the advice in this chapter, and you can cut your RVing expenses way down. And when you're not spending much money, you'll find that life is so much more enjoyable.

Chapter 9

How is it Possible to RV on $1,000 a Month?

"It's nice to get out of the rat race, but you have to learn to get along with less cheese."

~ Gene Perret

In this chapter, I will show you several examples of RVers living on $1,000 a month or less, but I'll be realistic and also give you examples of RVers who spend a little more than $1,000, although not a lot more.

To live on less than $1,000 a month it's almost a necessity that you be debt free—no credit card debt, no student loan debt, no car or truck payments, and no RV payments.

In reality, the money you're paying on debt is not part of your living expenses. That money is going towards paying for the living you've already done but didn't pay for while you were doing it. I'm not saying you shouldn't have incurred those debts. I'm just saying, "Call a spade a spade."

The idea of RVing on $1,000 a month or less sounds nice, but are people really doing it? Since seeing is believing, I have provided links below to a few short YouTube videos showing RVers who are actually doing it.

Examples of RVing on $1,000 a month

Youtube.com/watch?v=fvP2XHMDdE4&t=9s — In this video Kyle and Olivia talk about how much they spend living full time in their RV. They go a little over the $1,000 a month number and spend about $1,300 a month, but that includes making payments on some credit card debt and paying off a student loan. So, their actual cost to live in their RV is about $1,000 a month.

Youtube.com/watch?v=XL60tPbY2YE — Here is a link to Robin's video where she discusses her budget and explains how she lives on a little less than $1,300 a month. She also shows you where she could get her living expenses down to less than $1,000 a month. For example, she spends $400 on food for one person. She could cut some out of that for sure. I would assume that she is eating out a lot.

Youtube.com/watch?v=sKRY6dR7Ae4&t=202s — Eric shows how he lives full time in his Class C motorhome and spends $655 a month, and that includes $100 a month on his cat. Is he feeding that cat caviar? He doesn't show anything in the budget for maintenance, but he can add $100 or so for maintenance and still be well under $1,000 a month.

Youtube.com/watch?v=VduibSuyHA4 — Bill goes over five years of his expenses, and he spent a little over $1,000 a month, but as you can see he spent a lot of money on traveling and other things that you wouldn't spend if you were on a tight budget.

Youtube.com/watch?v=g_OmZzZD4rg — In this video Sam breaks down his monthly costs and shows how he spends $1,650 a month, with $330 for gas and $450 for campground fees. He could travel less and boondock and get his expenses below the $1,000 a month level.

Youtube.com/watch?v=VdZ0HWyoMjQ&t=11s — In this video Toby explains how he lives in a Ford Transit Connect van and spends $750 a month.

As you can see, some of the people in these videos are spending more than $1,000 a month, but I think you can see how it would be easy for them to get their expenses down to $1,000 a month.

Just because it's possible to live on less than $1,000 a month, it doesn't mean that you should or have to do it all the time. Just knowing that you can do it for a while if you need to—because of the loss of one of your sources of income or because of needing to build your emergency fund back up—gives you a lot of security.

Get rid of debt

If at all possible, get rid of all debt before you start living the RV lifestyle. If you have a student loan, you may not be able to pay that off immediately, but by all means get rid of your high interest rate credit card debt. Also, get rid of car payments. Either pay off the loan if there is not much left to pay or consider selling your car, paying off the loan and then getting a less expensive car. You're not trying to keep up with the Joneses anymore (or at least you shouldn't be).

Don't go into debt to buy your RV. Buy the RV that you can afford to pay cash for, and don't spend all of your cash. Any RV you buy will need some money spent on it. You will also need to keep some of your cash for an emergency fund. Don't think about hitting the road without an emergency fund.

And by all means, don't buy a new RV. Buying your RV will be discussed in Chapter 13.

To get rid of debt before you start living your RVing lifestyle it may mean that you will have to postpone your start date for a year or so—but it will be worth it. Your life will be a lot easier and simpler without debt.

Follow the steps discussed previously to get your living expenses down, then take the extra money and pay that debt off.

By the time you get your debt paid off, you will already be in the habit of living on a lot less money. That will make the transition to the RVing lifestyle a lot easier.

In addition to adjusting your lifestyle to save money as described in the previous chapter, here are some . . .

Other things you need to do to live on $1,000 a month

One of the most important things people who are living on $1,000 a month or less are doing is boondocking most of the time and not paying campground fees.

Camp for free

The United States government owns 47% of the land in the west. Most of it is controlled by the Bureau of Land Management (BLM). Most BLM land is available for camping for free. Usually, there is a 14-day limit, and then you have to move to another place, but a lot of times that is not enforced.

Not all free camping places are in the west

Free camping in the North Carolina mountains: I have camped on national forest land for a lot of nights in the North Carolina mountains. It's usually not free; most of the time it's $5.00 a night or $2.50 if you have the Senior Pass. They have the same 14-day limit on how long you can stay.

Free camping in Florida even in the winter time: I've found places in Florida to boondock and camp for free too. With all of the snowbirds in Florida in the winter you might think it's not possible to find free places to camp, but take a look at this 5-minute YouTube video and see how to find beautiful, free camping places in Florida.

Youtube.com/watch?v=IozjsDKupuc

Youtube.com/watch?v=fWTc8rm5nzAhow — Jason and Niki Wynn show us how they found some fabulous free camping places in Florida. Check out the Florida Water Management areas.

If you want to know more about how to find free places to boondock in Florida, check out this article by Jason and Niki:

GoneWithTheWynns.com/fabulous-free-camping-florida

Yes, you can camp all around the country and never have to pay a camping fee, but maybe a more practical approach (and what a lot of RVers do) is to boondock for two weeks and then stay in a full-hook-up campsite for a night or two. That way, they can dump their tanks, fill up with fresh water, charge their batteries, do laundry, and take a few long, hot showers. Then it's back to boondocking.

How to camp for half price

The nights you do stay in a full-hook-up campground, you don't always have to pay the full price. Sign up at Passport America.

PassportAmerica.com

For $44 a year you can stay at any one of over 2,000 campgrounds all around the country for half price. There are some restrictions, such as you can only stay for two or three nights and sometimes not on weekends, but you can work within these restrictions.

Sometimes these restrictions are negotiable. You're dealing directly with the campground, and if they're not busy, a lot of time you can stay longer than the published number of days or stay on a weekend if they're not full. Just ask.

When you're camping on BLM land and in national forests, you won't have electricity or a sewer dump. You will need a generator or solar. I found that, if I'm careful, I can go for the 14 days (which is the limit at a lot of BLM and national forest campsites) without having to dump my sewer and take on water.

There are several places that will let you dump your tanks and take on water. They usually charge $5.00 to $10.00. Most campgrounds and most Flying J truck stops offer this service. If you're a member of Camping World's Good Sam program, you can dump your tanks free at Camping World locations.

The best way to save on gas is not to travel as much. Duh, who figured that out?

I like to stay somewhere for two weeks to a month anyway. I don't like to travel every two or three days. Some people do. Doing that much traveling takes a lot of the joy out of RVing for me. I like to stop and smell the roses, check out the local area, and sample some of the local cuisine at a local mom and pop restaurant (not the expensive tourist or chain restaurants).

If you go into a chain restaurant, whether it's in Iowa or Georgia, they look the same. Why bother to travel?

As I've said before, I like to stay for a month in one place. If you're not boondocking and are paying to camp, one big advantage of staying for a month is that the monthly rate is about twice the weekly rate, so whether you stay for two weeks or a month, the price is the same.

Where I like to camp

There may not be any RVs in Heaven (but I can't understand why not). In the meantime, where can you RV that's close to Heaven?

Everyone has their opinion, and I disagree with most of them. If you follow many of the RVing bloggers and vloggers (a term that means video bloggers—in other words people who post videos on YouTube), you will see them raving about how beautiful the desert and western part of the US is.

The western part of the US has some breath-taking scenery.

If you haven't seen this part of the country, you're missing some interesting and unusual sights, but I sure wouldn't call the scenes beautiful.

I was watching one RVing video recently, and a lady was shooting her video with the desert behind her. There was nothing as far as you could see except dirt, sand, and some rolling hills. She was talking about how beautiful the scenery was. Give me a break.

Yes, it's interesting to visit these areas, but don't leave me there. I want to be around green mountains, waterfalls, rivers, and mountain streams. In other words, I want to be close to Heaven.

For the life of me, I can't understand how they can say that the desert is beautiful (except for a short period in the spring when the flowers are blooming). There are some great rock formations to see (and by all means see the Grand Canyon), but for me beautiful is not the word I would use to describe the Southwest.

I don't dislike the entire west. The Tetons, the waterfalls in Oregon, and some other places are nice. Just don't put me in the desert and try to tell me that it's beautiful.

An interesting observation. Have you ever noticed that almost all of the TV commercials for new cars, pickup trucks, and SUVs are filmed in the West? Just an observation. I guess they think it's beautiful too.

One of the big advantages of living in an RV is that home doesn't have to be just one place.

I don't like cold weather, and the mountains get cold and have snow during the winter months, so I head to Florida with the other snowbirds for four or five months in the winter. Florida gets way too hot for me during the summer months, but it sure is wonderful and warm in the winter.

I spend most of my time camping in different parts of the Appalachian Mountains—mainly in North Carolina, Tennessee, and Virginia. As far as I'm concerned, this is as close to Heaven as you can get in your RV. An added advantage is that the black bears you encounter in the eastern mountains are not vicious like the grizzly bears in the Rockies.

I've stepped out the door of my motorhome and been face-to-face with a black bear more than once. It's interesting that I've seen more bears inside the city limits of small towns in the mountains than I have out in the wild. Maybe it's because the bears know that it's against the law to fire a gun inside the city limits, so they are safe, but if they are out in the wild, they could get shot.

There was a big mama bear and her two cubs on my brother's front porch last week. Yes, he lives in the mountains, too, but in a house.

I put up with (and respect) black bears in the North Carolina mountains just like I did alligators for 20 years when I lived on Hilton Head Island in South Carolina, but I wouldn't want to try to live around grizzly bears. They're too vicious for me.

Let all of the RV bloggers keep telling the world how wonderful and beautiful the western part of the US is for RVing. If everyone keeps believing that and most of the RVers stay in the West, that's fine with me. It'll make it easier for me to find available campsites in my Appalachian Mountains.

And who knows, since I'm so close to Heaven here, one day I might just get to sneak my RV into Heaven.

I was telling a fellow RVer who was not used to driving in the mountains this recently, and he said, "Yeah, I can see how driving a Class A motorhome through these mountains on these crooked roads could get you into Heaven (or somewhere else) pretty easily."

Stop buying stuff

One of the best ways to get your living expenses down is to stop buying stuff. Going shopping should no longer be a form of entertainment. In addition to saving a lot of money, another reason to stop buying things is that when you live in an RV, you don't have room for stuff.

Adopt the habit of getting rid of something every time you buy something new. If you buy a new pair of shoes, throw out an old pair. When you're considering buying something, ask yourself, "What am I going to throw away?" That may keep you from buying the item being considered.

I don't mean you should just cut back. I'm saying that you should stop buying stuff altogether (well almost).

Save money on clothes

When you're living in an RV, you don't have room for a lot of clothes. You probably have enough clothes to last you a long time before you will ever need to buy more.

And when you do need more clothes, go to Goodwill or a thrift shop. There was a time when people tried to keep it a secret that they shopped at Goodwill. Now they brag about it. I was sitting around a campfire not long ago and one woman commented to another woman that she liked her shirt. Her reply was, "I got it at Goodwill for $4.00."

An RVing friend of mine's father died recently. He had gotten rid of all of his suits and sports coats when he started RVing. He went to Goodwill and paid $5.00 for a sports coat to wear to his father's funeral and then on the way home from the funeral he stopped and donated it back to Goodwill.

There's no room in an RV for clothes (or anything else) that you don't use often.

Healthcare—the elephant in the room

Depending on your age and situation, you may think that the cost of healthcare could make your dream of living on $1,000 a month impossible.

But maybe not. Now, there are options. In Chapter 14 I go into your healthcare options in great detail and provide links to articles and websites that will show you how to cut your healthcare costs and get healthcare down to a manageable number—maybe even to almost zero.

Bottom line: Get out of debt and change your lifestyle (as described in this chapter), and you can easily live on less than $1,000 a month. Check out the links provided earlier in the chapter where RVers show you their itemized monthly expenses and how they live on less than $1,000 a month. This will prove to you that it can be done.

Chapter 10

Learn to RV on $1K a month, Then Find a Way to Make More

"Life does not get better by chance, it gets better by change."

~ Jim Rohn

Hopefully, the previous chapters have convinced you that you can live full time in your RV on $1,000 a month. I've given you several examples of people who are doing it.

So, I think you can see that it's not a matter of whether it's possible or not. It comes down to—do you want to live that lifestyle?

Yes, learning to live on $1,000 a month will take some adjusting. It's like learning to live on a new diet. It will be hard to do, and it won't seem normal for a while. But after you get used to the new way of living, it will start to come naturally.

Here's an alternative

If money is tight, prove to yourself that you can live on $1,000 a month, and then find a way to make more money. Just because you can live on $1,000 a month, it doesn't mean that you have to or even that you should.

If you're living on $5,000 a month, adding another $500 a month to your budget probably won't make much difference in your lifestyle. But if you're living on $1,000 a month, adding another $500 to your budget will make a big difference.

And if you can find a way to raise your income by $500 a month, you can probably find a way to raise it by $1,000. I'll talk about that in the next chapter.

It gives you a lot of peace of mind to know that you can always go back to living on $1,000 a month—even if it's only for a short time.

I spoke previously about the importance of having an emergency fund. But if you have to use your emergency fund, it's good to know that can you go back to living on

$1,000 a month for a few months while you build your emergency fund back up, and then you can change back to living on a larger monthly budget like you were before the emergency. Not being prepared for an emergency can kill your RVing dreams.

When it comes to finding a way to make more money, the techniques described in the next chapter cover literally hundreds of ways RVers make money while living on the road. This is not just theory. The techniques described in the next chapter are all being used by RVers to earn more money.

Examples of RVers making money while RVing

YouTube.com/watch?v=ebbo800_Rg0 — This is one of my favorite videos. This 11-minute video interview is with a young, single, female, solo RVer. She has now been on the road for six years and earns the money to support her lifestyle in a variety of ways. Her 16-foot camper may seem small, but she has now bought an even smaller camper and is waiting for delivery. Her story will inspire you to hit the road, and it will convince you that you can do it too. (I referenced this video in a previous chapter, but I know that a lot of people skip over the videos I link to, so I'm providing this link again in this chapter. I really think it's worth watching.)

YouTube.com/watch?v=YF8bEvCBiyw — Eight tips for finding online work. There is a follow-up video referenced in this video that shows you how to make money off-line without a computer.

This chapter is not intended to show you how to find a lot of ways to make more money on the road. That is covered in great detail in the next chapter. The purpose of this chapter is to convince you that you can do it (and that you should do it). Your life on the road will be so much more enjoyable if you have a little more than $1,000 a month coming in.

But I do think it's important to first convince yourself that you really can live on $1,000 a month.

Bottom line: I think you can learn to live on $1,000 a month, but you have to prove it to yourself, so you'll believe it. Then it's important that you find a way to make even more money. It's always a good idea to have more than one stream of income. A stream of income can dry up at the drop of a hat. You don't ever want to be in a position where the loss of a stream of income jeopardizes your RVing lifestyle.

Chapter 11

How RVers Make Money on the Road

"I looked up my family tree and found out I was the sap."

~ Rodney Dangerfield

There are so many options for how RVers can make money now that a whole book could be written about how to do—oh wait, a book has just been written about how RVers make money on the road.

It was written by William Myers, author of the popular series of RVing adventure novels in the Mango Bob series.

By the way, the latest book in that series is called *Mango Digger* and it's my favorite of all of the books in the series.

Back to making money on the road, the book I am talking about is called *Road Cash*. That's a fitting title because that's what the book is all about. The book came out not long ago and is up to date. It goes into great detail about more ways that RVers are actually making money while living on the road than you could ever imagine.

In one of my previous books, I describe the seven ways I make money on the road, but that's only a drop in the bucket compared to what is revealed in this book.

If you're even remotely thinking about living in an RV, invest $3.99 and download this eBook. You can find it on Amazon at the link below:

Amazon.com/dp/B0721832MD

A printed version of the book is available also, but I like the eBook version, so I can click on the links without having to type them. And, trust me, you will want to check out the many links provided in the book.

The book describes ways RVers are making money using their computers and ways they are making money without using a computer.

The techniques described in this book are not ideas about how you might make money, but rather, the book describes the techniques RVers are actually using to make money and support their lifestyle.

Here's how the book is described on Amazon

"If you've dreamed of living on the road in an RV, Camper, or Van, but wondered how you could afford to do it, this book is for you.

"In Road Cash, you'll discover different ways to generate decent income while living on the road. You'll learn how to camp for free, how to build a steady income, how to make quick cash when you need it, and how to enjoy your life on the road while earning enough to pay your way.

"If you currently live on the road or are thinking about it, you'll want this book!"

You need multiple sources of income

I firmly believe that you need multiple sources of income if you're living on the road. Heck, my opinion is that you need more than one source of income even if you're not living on the road.

If you only have one source of income and it goes away (and it can in a heartbeat), you're up the creek. I don't want to jeopardize my lifestyle by relying on just one source of income.

Some sources of income take time before the money starts coming in (such as writing a book, producing videos, etc.), and some sources start producing income immediately. I think it's good to have both types of income.

How I make money on the road

Here is a brief description of the seven ways I've used over the last six years to make money on the road. In the list, I also tell you the pitfalls to look out for with each technique. At the end of the list, I'll tell you the two most profitable moneymaking techniques I'm using now that are making me the most money for the time invested.

1. **I buy closeout items from retail stores (Walmart, Kohl's, etc.) and sell them on Amazon.** One thing to look out for is that a lot of the closeout items (particularly toys) are returned items and sometimes pieces are missing. If I see signs that the box has been opened, I don't buy the item.

2. **I buy items from China and sell them on Amazon.** I sold over $100,000 worth of items this way one year according to the 1099 Form I received from Amazon. It was a lot of work and, even though there were a lot of sales, the profit margin was small.

3. **Have ad-supported websites.** I made $1,700 one month using this technique, but Amazon and eBay don't pay

as much now as they used to. Also, Google has made it harder to get these types of websites ranked high.

4. **Subscription websites.** These can be profitable if you have the right topic. I used to have three subscription websites. Now I only have one **(LifeRV.com)** and right now it's free to join, so it's not bringing in income. I may later convert it and start charging a monthly fee to join.

5. **Provide in-room directories to hotels and motels.** I still do this for a few hotels. It's profitable, but it involves selling ads to restaurants and sometimes it's hard to catch the restaurant owners in. The project brings in a few thousand a year plus a lot of the restaurants pay with gift certificates, so I can go out to eat a lot without any cash out of my pocket (except tips for the wait staff, which I do with cash). If you want to know all of the details of how this project works, see my book, *Young RVers*, available on Amazon at this link for $3.99. **Amazon.com/dp/0984496858**

6. **Writing books and selling them on Amazon.** This is by far the most profitable project I have for the time spent, and it brings in the most total income. The thing I like best about this project is that I do the work once and it continues to bring in income year after year. I use Amazon to sell the eBooks and I use **CreateSpace.com** in Charleston, South Carolina (which is now owned by Amazon), to print and deliver the printed books to

Amazon. If you haven't published a book before, start by writing a how-to book. They don't sell as well as novels, but they're so much easier and faster to write.

7. **Posting Videos on YouTube.** I'm just getting started on this project. I like it because, like writing books, you do the work once and get paid year after year. There's a lot to learn—not only about how to shoot and edit videos but also about how to rank high on YouTube's list of videos. The good news is there are a lot of videos on YouTube showing you how to do all of these things.

More examples of RVers making money

Below are some links to YouTube videos where RVers talk about the ways they are making money while living full time on the road. Watch these videos and I think you can get some ideas about how you can make money on the road.

Keep in mind that, even if you don't have the skills required to do one of the jobs you find interesting, with all of the books and videos available, you can learn how to do almost any job in a short amount of time. You don't have to be an expert to start earning an income doing something. You just need to be a little better at it than the average person—and that's not hard to do in a lot of cases.

An article and two videos about making money while RVing

ThePennyHoarder.com/make-money/wfh/working-and-living-in-an-rv — This article has some valuable information including links to CBS News articles and other sources.

Youtube.com/watch?v=fz9lUfeal60 — In this 15-minute video Toby explains how he gets jobs making up to $18 an hour.

Youtube.com/watch?v=NGxmSGf2Kr8 — In this 14-minute video 17 full-time RVers explain how they make money on the road. It's a real eye-opener.

Youtube.com/watch?v=Gnr2N__mdSY — This 10-minute video features seven full-time RVers explaining how they make money and live full time in their RVs. (Note: When typing this link there are two underline characters together between the "N" and the "m" in this URL.)

Making money while living on the road has never been easier. In fact, even a few years ago, many of the techniques RVers use to make money were not even possible.

Bottom line: There's no one technique that's right for everybody, but look at all of the income producing techniques described in this chapter (including the ones described in the *Road Cash* book) and see if you don't find

several that match your skills and interest and will allow
you to make a lot more than the $1,000 a month you will
need to support your RVing lifestyle.

Chapter 12

Grow Your Skill Set and Make Even More

"Be yourself; everyone else is already taken."

~ Oscar Wilde

Until you quit your job (or retired) and hit the road, you probably didn't have much time to learn a new skill or a need to do it. Now you're in a whole different world—a wonderful and fun world, but a different world.

The previous chapter talked about ways RVers make money on the road, and the book I referenced in that chapter goes into great detail showing hundreds of ways RVers are actually making money on the road.

You might be thinking that you don't have the knowledge or skills to do most of those jobs. You don't want to do most of them—you just need to do one (or two or three).

One of the keys to making more money on the road is to grow your skill set.

For example, you may think that you're not good with computers. You don't need to be. You only need to be reasonably good at using one program—video editing, graphic design, etc.

There are YouTube videos that teach you step by step how to do almost anything. You could hold up in a campground (or boondock) for a week and, even though you may not master the program, you can get to a functional level and be ready to start using your new skill to make money. You'll get better and more skilled as you start working with the program.

You can do this for a lot of different skills. Before you hit the road, you probably didn't have time to learn new skills, but now you do.

One of the most important things is to be sure you're learning skills that you're interested in. Don't try to learn to be a great photographer if you're not interested in it.

While you're at it, remember that you can learn some skills that you don't plan to use to make money. Maybe you want to learn to play the guitar or learn to paint with watercolors, etc. Now you have the time to do it.

Back to making money

The ideal thing is to find something you can learn that you're interested in and something that pays good money.

You don't have to be an expert at something to make money doing it. You only have to be a little better than most people, and for many (if not most) things that's not hard to do.

It's like the old joke about two guys hiking in the woods. One of them asked the other one, "What are you going to do if a bear starts to chase us?" The other one answered, "I'm going to run." The first one said, "You can't outrun a bear." The guy said, "I don't have to outrun the bear. All I have to do is outrun you."

Don't rule something out just because you're not good at it or don't know how to do it. You can learn.

Here are some examples

How about learning to be a house-painter, bartender or waitress or waiter? If you're going to be in one place for a month or so at a time, it's possible to get a job working a few hours a week and make good money. Cleaning houses is another way RVers make money, and there's not much learning required to do it. An RVer I parked next to recently cleans houses. She charges $25 an hour, and she is booked up, and has a waiting list.

I know people who are doing this and enjoy it. They get to meet the locals and learn about interesting things to see and do in the area—and, of course, they make some good money by working just a few hours.

Two types of moneymaking projects

I think jobs working on the road fit into one of two categories. One is work that gives you an immediate income, like being a waiter, waitress, bartender, or music teacher, cleaning houses, or doing yard work, etc.

I have one friend who posts on Craigslist that he is available to do handyman work, and he gets all the work he wants.

Then there's work that you do where you hope to get paid in the future. Writing books, creating and posting videos on YouTube, starting a website or blog, etc.

The type of work you choose to do will depend on your situation. If you need money immediately to live on, you don't want to be spending your time writing a book. The book you write might bring in a lot of money or almost no money at all, but whatever it does, it won't do it immediately.

I think maybe the ideal thing is to work on some of both kinds of projects. It's always good to have more than one source of income. It's also good to have something that's bringing in immediate income and then, if you have time, work on a project that will bring in a lot of money for the time spent, but at a later date.

If you're going to be in an area for a month or more, it's usually easy to find jobs, but there are jobs that you can find even if you're only going to be in an area for a day or two.

I have a friend who plays the guitar and sings. He has been able to find one-night gigs in almost any town he is in. He has references that restaurants and bars can call to check him out. He said that if he can get the manager to call one or more of his references, he almost always gets the job.

Having references that people can call always helps you get the job, whether you're playing music, being a waitress, fixing computers, or just about anything else.

So, by all means, develop a list of references you can use, and in most cases that will almost certainly clinch your job-hunting chore.

Be open to doing jobs you have never done or even thought about doing before and you could find them fun and interesting. I have friends who have done things such as being a host and caretaker at a lighthouse, working in a gift shop at a national park, working as a landscape assistant—the list goes on and on.

Note that the jobs I'm talking about are different from workamping jobs where you get a free campsite in exchange for doing some work. A lot of RVers do workamping in addition to other jobs.

One moneymaking task almost everyone should be working on

When you write a book, you get paid month after month, year after year, for a very long time.

A novel is a lot harder to write than a how-to book, and a novel takes a lot longer to write. Even if you don't know anything about writing, there are lots of books available on Amazon that will teach you how to develop all of the skills you need to know.

If you're going to write a novel, you'll need to know how to develop a plot, how to develop characters, how to write dialog, etc. Don't worry about grammar. Write like you would talk. In fact, you could use a program like Dragon Naturally Speaking that will convert speech into text. A lot of writers use this technique. Then all you have to do is tell a story.

You can find people online who will do the proofreading, editing, formatting, cover design, etc. Go to **Fiverr.com** and find the help you need. The cost is extremely reasonable for the work they do.

By the way, later, if you learn to do the editing, formatting, cover design, proofreading, etc., yourself, that's another set of skills you can use to make money. Sign up with Fiverr.com and do the work for other people.

One word of advice. Don't depend on yourself to do your own proofreading. You can proofread your book a dozen times (and you should), but there will still be typos and grammar problems. All writers know they can't catch all of their own errors.

I can't write, but I support my RVing lifestyle writing books

I'm an engineer. I kid you not; I never got an "A" or even a "B" in a single college English class in my life. I was happy to get a "C" because I didn't know grammar, I couldn't write, and I didn't like English classes. I'm still not very good at grammar or how to write. I just write like I talk.

The good news is I don't have to be good with grammar or all of that writing technique stuff. I find freelance experts on **Fiverr.com** to fix all of my mistakes, and the reader never knows that I am incompetent when it comes to writing.

That's the technique I've used to write and publish the 12 books I've written. And by the way, the monthly income from the books pays all of my expenses of living on the road.

You don't have to write a great book. Your goal in writing your first book should be to follow Larry the Cable Guy's advice and just, "Git-R-Done." Writing your second book will be a lot easier.

What should you do after you write a book? Write another book.

Bottom line: Step outside your comfort zone and learn a new skill. I think you will find it both fun and profitable. When you're living on the road, it's important to have more than one stream of income.

Chapter 13

How to Buy a Reliable RV at a Great Price

"It is good to have an end to journey toward; but it is the journey that matters, in the end."

~ Ernest Hemingway

RVs sell for prices that range from one thousand dollars to over one million dollars. Actually, some sell for up to two or three million dollars, but we won't spend time talking about those. If you could afford one of those, you wouldn't be reading this book. But they are fun to walk through when you're attending RV shows.

Let's get back down to earth. All of our lives we've wanted bigger, fancier, and better things.

It's easy for that habit to carry over into how we go about selecting an RV. I bought a 34-foot Class A motorhome, which is way bigger than I need just for me. I don't even have a dog, so I for sure don't need an RV this big.

If I were going to be boondocking in some remote places, it would really be too big, but since I don't boondock in places that are hard to get to, it's not a big deal. I do enjoy the space this big RV gives me, so I'm not going to get rid of the motorhome I have now and get another one anytime soon. I've made a lot of modifications to it and added a lot of gadgets to it, and I'm happy with it. It's like one of the family now.

Which type of RV is best for full-time living?

Everyone who is considering the RV lifestyle spends a lot of time stressing out over what type of RV they should buy. There are motorhomes, fifth-wheels, travel trailers, and then, when it comes to motorhomes, there are Class A, Class B, Class C, and converted vans and buses—the list goes on.

And to make the choice even harder, all these different types of RVs come in a variety of different lengths.

It's only natural that if it's going to be your home, you want to make the right choice. In other words, you want to pick the perfect RV for you and for your lifestyle, but that's impossible.

The problem is there's no one type of RV that's perfect for the RVing lifestyle. And even if there were an RV that's perfect for you, you wouldn't know how to find it or even be able to recognize it if you did find it. Here's why:

- You don't know much about RVs or what kind you would be happy with.

- You don't know much about how or where you'll be traveling.

- And even if you did know all of this, more than likely, your wants will change after you start RVing.

Your first RV is not going to be the right one

Accept the fact that the first RV you buy is not going to be the right one for you and your family, so stop worrying about it. Enjoy your first RV, learn from it, and then you will be ready to get your next RV that will be closer to what you want and need for you and your family.

Two years ago, a friend of mine sold his house and decided to live and travel full time in an RV. The one thing he was sure about was that he didn't want to do any boondocking.

He wanted to always be in an RV park with full hook-ups (water, electric, and sewer).

Since he was so sure that this is what he wanted to do, he bought a camper that didn't have holding tanks.

I'm sure you're already ahead of me, but he soon decided that he loved boondocking. That's all he wants to do. So now he has bought another camper with solar, and, of course, holding tanks.

Leave your check book at home (so you can't be talked into buying something) and visit some RV dealers. Go inside several RVs (Class A, B, and C, fifth-wheels, campers, etc.). Look at the floor plan, sit on the couch, sit on the john, and stretch out across the bed. In other words, picture yourself living in that RV. Be sure to check out the different sizes of each type of RV.

After you have what I call your first guess as to what would be the ideal RV for you and your lifestyle (we both know it probably won't be the RV you will have or want in a year or two), your next step is to do your research and find out what the fair market value is.

Of course, that's not the price you want to pay. You want to buy an RV for less than it's worth. But you can't do that until you do enough research to actually know what a certain type of RV is worth.

As my father always told me, you make your money when you buy something—not when you sell it. You can expect to sell it for about what it's worth. Your goal is to buy it for less than it's worth.

How do you find out the true market value of an RV?

You can't recognize a bargain when you find it if you don't know the true market value of the type of RV you're looking for. So, after you have an idea of what type of RV you want, you need to find out what the fair market value of that RV is.

Here are some sources that can give you that information:

First, don't go by the asking price or sticker price of the used RVs on dealers' lots. Many times, they will drop the asking price by 1/3 or more when you get down to some serious negotiating.

Below is a link to a website that shows what RVs have recently sold for.

Pplmotorhomes.com/sold/soldmenu.htm

The people at PPL Motorhomes sell about 4,000 motorhomes a year, and they show you what each one actually sold for. They also always have a huge inventory of used RVs for sale. Most of them are on consignment.

Another way to see what RVs are actually selling for is to check eBay and look at RVs that actually sold. Don't pay any attention to the asking prices. The sold price is the only price that matters.

Selecting the right RV

There are a lot of videos with advice about which type of RV is best for full-time living. Obviously, there's no one right type of RV. You will find people enjoying RVing full time in every type of RV you can imagine.

And if you ask them, most of them will tell you that they love their RV. In other words, you can't get an unbiased opinion of which type of RV is the best by asking RV owners.

First of all, buy an RV that you can afford to pay cash for if at all possible. Don't worry about finding the perfect RV. Within a year or two you will want to sell it and get a different one. I know I've said that before, but I want it to sink in. It's important that you actually believe this.

My opinion

In a nutshell, for full-time RV living, I would recommend going with an RV like the one I have. (Of course, most other RVers will tell you the same thing—that is, go with an RV like the one they have.)

In other words, a used (and it can be very used) Class A with two slides (unless you plan on doing a lot of boondocking in rough terrain or you're going to be a solo RVer).

One of the main advantages of a Class A is that it has a lot of storage space in what is called the "basement," which is the storage bins under the RV. I guess that's why that space is called the basement. Other classes of motorhomes and campers don't have that space. Fifth-wheel RVs do have more storage than the other RVs, but not as much as a Class A.

A Class A RV does not have much ground clearance, so you have to be careful when you're boondocking. There are a lot of boondocking places you can't get to in a Class A.

A Class A is not the right choice for everyone and maybe not the right choice for you. Do your research and legwork.

Campers (or travel trailers) are a good option to consider

They have better ground clearance and can get into more boondocking places than a Class A or even a Class C motorhome.

A lot of people love camper/trailers. Nathan and Marissa have had four different RVs (a Class A, a fifth-wheel, and two campers) since they started RVing four years ago. Now they have an Airstream camper and love it. They say it's just right for their family of three and the way they travel and camp. They like to boondock a lot in remote areas. Check out their YouTube channel at *Less Junk-More Journey*.

If you're traveling solo, you could look at Class C RVs or maybe even a van. Class B RVs are small, easy to drive, and get good gas mileage. They are very popular, and that makes them expensive.

If you're on a tight budget and plan to live in your RV full time, I wouldn't recommend a Class B, but I have a lot of friends who have them and love them. As Shakespeare said, "To each his own."

There's no right way to RV, and for sure there's no RV that's right for everyone or for every type of RVing.

Some people recommend going with a diesel engine. They have a lot more power, but they are more expensive to buy and more expensive to maintain. With my gas engine, I have to go slow up mountains, but I'm not in that big of a hurry. If I were going to be traveling a lot in the Rockies, I might wish I had the power of a diesel engine.

There are advantages and disadvantages to the other types of RVs. The Class C motorhomes are easier to drive and get a little better gas mileage. They have more ground clearance, which would be better for boondocking, but there is not much storage. If you're going to live in your RV full time, you'll appreciate the extra storage space that a Class A RV has.

A lot of people love the Class B RVs and vans, and they would work well for one person, especially if you were going to be traveling a lot or doing a lot of boondocking.

The fifth-wheel campers have more room. If you have kids, this could come in handy. You could have a bedroom up front and another bedroom or bunk beds in the back. They are easier to tow than a camper/trailer.

The only thing that really matters when selecting an RV is to buy one you can afford, and to buy one that you can sell in a year or so that you can at least get your money back and maybe even make a profit on.

As you can see, there's no one type of RV that's right for all situations and lifestyles. The real answer is to listen to Lidia's advice on her YouTube channel *SimpleRVing*. She says, "Listen to your soul. Simplify and go."

Is it possible to get a really low-cost RV that's functional?

I know a lot of people who have hit the road in RVs that they paid $5,000 to $10,000 for and sometimes even less.

Here's an example of someone spending even less. Brett bought a 1985 Coachman Class C motorhome recently for $800 and hit the road. He drove it 1,000 miles on his first trip, and everything worked fine. He has been living in it now for over a year, and everything is still working.

Below is a link to a video of him describing his $800 motorhome.

Youtube.com/watch?v=T_EoN9AkRek

Below are two links to Class A motorhomes that were purchased for $500 each.

Youtube.com/watch?v=n6_opku2Iik&t=28s

Youtube.com/watch?v=ITR6EmsW7ks

When you're buying a used RV (whether you're paying $1,000 or $100,000), be sure to check the date code on the tires. Don't look at the tread on the tires like you would if you were buying a used car.

It's okay to buy an RV when the tires are almost aged out, but make sure you know this and plan to spend $3,000 or so for tires soon after you buy the RV. In other words, factor that cost into the price you're paying and see if you still like the deal.

RV tires don't wear out, they age out

Ozone and UV light cause a tire to deteriorate. (It's called dry rot.) RV tires are good for seven or eight years. After that, tires will start to crack and become dangerous to drive on.

To tell the age of the tires on the RV you're looking at, look for the 4-digit date code on the tires (sometimes it's on the inside and you have to crawl under the RV to see it). It's the last four digits in the series of numbers and letters that start with "DOT" as shown in the photo below.

The first two digits are the week and the second two are the year the tire was manufactured. The tire in the photo was made in the third week of 2013.

This tire was manufactured in the third week of 2013

You have to negotiate when buying an RV

Some people don't like to negotiate and some people who do like to negotiate do it all wrong. In other words, they're not very good at it—some people who think they're good negotiators get taken to the cleaners.

Negotiating doesn't have to be a hassle or an unpleasant experience. Just use one or more of the seven statements below and watch the asking price start to decrease in a hurry. If you use these statements, negotiating can be a fun experience.

Here are my 7 all-time favorite negotiating phrases for people who don't like to negotiate

1. ALWAYS, ALWAYS flinch at the first price or proposal.

2. Next, when you get the lower price quote, you should say, "You've got to do better than that."

3. If you make a counter offer, always ask for a much lower price than you expect to get.

4. Never offer to split the difference. The other party is almost always willing to do that, so try to get a slightly better deal than that.

5. Use two powerful negotiating techniques in one sentence. The two techniques are "Absent higher authority," and "If I could, would you?" We've all experienced the "Absent higher authority" technique. For example, "Our insurance regulations won't let you go back in the shop," or "The loan committee wouldn't go along with those terms." Here's how to use the technique in your favor for once. When you're down to the final negotiations, you can say, "If I could get my (financial adviser, spouse or some absent higher

authority) to go along with this, would you replace the two front tires?"

6. Nibble for more at the end. You can usually get a little bit more even after you have basically agreed on everything. You can say, "You ARE going to have the carpets professionally cleaned (or you are going to replace the windshield wiper blades), aren't you?"

7. When you're getting close to the end of the negotiations and everything is just about nailed down, say, "I'm getting nervous about this," and then SHUT UP. A lot of times this technique will get you one more concession. This technique works really well when a woman says it, because men have a tendency to believe women change their minds sometimes for no logical reason. (I wonder why men think that.)

If you follow the information in this chapter, you can end up with an RV that's right for you and for thousands of dollars less than you would spend if you went the conventional route of buying an RV.

After a year on the road you will want a different RV

Finding and buying your first RV is a simple process since you only have one criterion. That one criterion is to find an RV that you can sell in a year or so for at least what you paid for it and hopefully even more. In other words, one you can sell in a year or so and make a profit on.

The reason is simple, over half of the people I know who live in an RV sell their first one within a year or two and get a different one. And even more people wish they could, but they bought a new RV, and they would lose their shirt if they sold their new RV after only having it for a year or so.

Summary of how to find and buy your first RV

The simple answer is to do enough soul-searching and research to decide what type of RV you think you want, do research to determine what a fair price would be for the RV you want, and then do your research to find that RV at a price that is less than a fair price. You want a bargain. Keep looking until you find it.

One final point: Before you buy any RV, spend the $200 to $500 or more (depending on the level of inspection you want) to have it inspected. Even after you have already settled on the price, you can usually negotiate the price down enough to more than cover the inspection cost by bringing up the things the inspector found that you didn't know when you agreed on the price.

You can find certified RV inspectors in your area at **nrvia.org/locate.** Another option is to get a local RV mechanic to do the inspection for you.

Bottom line: Do your research to determine what type of RV will be best for you. Next look at your budget and the cash you have available. Then use the methods described in this chapter to find the RV you're looking for—and be sure to use some or all of the negotiating techniques I've outlined to get an even better deal.

Chapter 14

Domicile, Mail, Healthcare, Internet, Banking, Pets, and Kids

"The art of medicine consists of amusing the patient while nature cures the disease."

~Voltaire

You have probably been giving a lot of thought and time to some of what are considered the bigger problems and tasks required to hit the road and live full time in an RV— things like finding and buying the right RV, selling your house, getting rid of most of your stuff, etc.

Of course, these big things are important, but there are some little things that are important too. Here are some tasks that don't take much time, but they are easy to put off. And sometimes you can completely forget to take care of them.

Don't fall into the trap of putting these things off. Make a list and start knocking them out.

Seven little things to take care of before you hit the road

- In which state is your domicile? In other words, where do you legally live?

- How to get your mail.

- How to get healthcare.

- How to stay connected to the internet.

- How to handle your banking.

- What about pets?

- How to RV with kids.

Don't worry. You're not the first person to have to deal with these things. Other full-time RVers have already solved these problems.

The good news is that there are simple solutions to each of the things I've listed. In the rest of this chapter, I will show you how other RVers have handled each of these problems.

In which state is your domicile (where do you legally live)?

This is the first thing you need to take care of. You can't decide how to get your mail, how to get healthcare, and a lot of other things until you decide where you legally and officially live (even though you may not physically be there very often).

Since you'll probably be rambling all over the US (or at least in several different states), where do you legally live? You can't just say, "Everywhere," even though that might be the correct answer.

You have to declare a state and say it is your domicile, and you have to have a physical address in that state.

Before you can get your driver's license and register your car and motorhome, etc., you have to select a state to call home.

Since it's free to select any state, most people choose either Texas, Florida or South Dakota because there is no state income tax in these states (along with several other reasons).

There are other states with no income tax, but, for several reasons, Texas and Florida are the two states most RVers choose.

South Dakota used to be a popular state, but they have changed some laws, and it's no longer a good choice in my opinion, particularly if you're not on Medicare.

After you select your domicile state, you will have to do things just as you would if you actually moved there—get a local address, get your driver's license issued in that state, register your vehicles, change your address with all your credit cards, banks, register to vote, etc. It's not hard, just a lot of little things to do.

Here is a link to a 43-minute YouTube video by Bob Wells:

Youtube.com/watch?v=jntFI_5FiA8&t=13s He gives a detailed explanation of your domicile state options and he goes over several things you will want to consider before you select your domicile state. It's a long video and maybe you don't want to know that much about the topic right now, but, at some point, before you make your decision, I would recommend you watch the video.

By the way, the choice Bob made for where to call home works for him (and he explains why), but for most people, I would recommend Florida or Texas.

Keep in mind that out of the three main full-time residency states (Florida, Texas, and South Dakota) only Florida has

Obamacare plans that provide nationwide coverage (Florida Blue). This may change for 2019, but hopefully not.

Be careful if you live in an aggressive tax state

If you presently live in an aggressive tax state (such as New York, California, Illinois, etc.), and if there is a lot of tax involved, these states may come after you and try to claim that you are still a resident of their state and therefore owe them tax revenue. In some cases, they have been successful at this.

It comes down to which state you plan to eventually live in. It might be hard to convince tax authorities that you plan to live permanently in South Dakota when you have only been there once in five years.

After considering all of these options, I would suggest that you seriously consider Florida as your domicile state, but it's not the best option for everyone. Consider everything that's been presented here, do your research to see how the rules have changed, and then make your decision.

One other option (and the one a lot of people choose) is to do nothing and keep your domicile state the same as it is now. In other words, use a friend or relative's address or set up a UPS box as your official address.

That's what I did. I left my domicile state as North Carolina. My brother picks up my mail for me about once a month and lets me know if there is anything important (like a summons for jury duty, etc.).

If you plan on going back to your present home state often, this might be the best choice. After all, you can see your same doctors, dentist, auto mechanic, and old friends, etc., on your return visits.

By the way, the State of North Carolina would not let me use my UPS box as the address on my driver's license. Their computer kicked it out, so I had to use my brother's address. No big problem. Just one more hoop to have to jump through.

I still have to pay North Carolina state income tax. I might decide to change to Florida one of these days, but for the last six years, I have continued to officially live in North Carolina.

One of the reasons I have been thinking about establishing my official domicile state as Florida is that, in addition to not having to pay any state income tax, Florida residents can stay in Florida state parks for half price. Half price would be $8 to $21 a night depending on the park, and that price usually includes water and electricity.

Another reason I haven't changed yet is that it's expensive the first year to transfer vehicle registrations (motorhome and car) to Florida. But after the first year, it's relatively inexpensive.

How do you get your mail?

After you select a state to call home, you will need an address in that state, so you need to establish an address with a friend or a mail forwarding service.

If you have a friend or relative in the state you select, you might want to consider using them and their address to save a little money.

Here are some links to recommended mail forwarding services in each of the three common states people choose as their domicile. Contact them and they can give you many more details.

Florida:

SbiMailService.com

Escapees.com/mail-services

MyRvMail.com

AmHomeBase.com

Texas:

Escapees.com/mail-services

South Dakota:

Americas-Mailbox.com

Escapees.com/mail-services

These mail forwarding services charge a small monthly fee (about $12 to $15 a month) depending on the services you want them to perform. For example, they will forward all of your mail when you request it (weekly, monthly, etc.). You will also have to give them an address each time you want your mail forwarded.

They also offer a service to scan the outside of your mail and email the scans to you and then you can tell them which pieces to forward and which ones to trash.

For an extra fee, they will even open your mail and scan the contents and forward that to you.

I would suggest you take steps to eliminate as much of your snail mail as possible. It just makes life easier. One easy way to eliminate a lot of unwanted mail is not to file a forwarding address with your current post office. Give your new address only to the people and businesses you want to have it.

Now that you've decided on your domicile state, you need to take the necessary steps to get an address set up in that state. You have to do this before you can start getting healthcare set up.

Then you can start getting your vehicle registration, driver's license, and insurance changed over and, of course, start jumping through the hoops to get health insurance, which I will describe in the next chapter—but you have to select a domicile state and have an address before you can do any of this.

Of course, be sure to change your address with the IRS, your banks, your eBay account, Amazon, and anywhere else that's important.

How will you get healthcare?

When it comes to living on $1,000 a month, one of the first things you have to think about is what you are going to do about healthcare. Some couples spend close to $1,000 a month just on health insurance and co-pays.

Some young people I know who are healthy, gamble and just pay their own medical bills and don't have health insurance. That approach saves them a lot of money, and for some people it works out okay, but it's a gamble. They are also gambling that the government doesn't start enforcing the penalty of $695 per adult or 2.5% of your annual income for not having insurance.

Paying cash can sometimes get you big discounts

I was talking with a friend yesterday and he told me about a situation he experienced one time when his wife had to go to the hospital for a minor procedure. The bill was $6,000. He told the hospital he didn't have insurance and that he would make them a one-time offer. He would pay them $1,500 cash right there on the spot to pay the bill in full.

They said they couldn't accept that. He got up and said, "Then I'm not going to pay the bill and good luck trying to collect." And he walked out.

They followed him out to the parking lot and when he was getting ready to get into his car, they said, "We'll take the $1,500."

I'm not saying you should be a deadbeat and not pay your bills, but be aware that medical expenses are negotiable. If you walk into a doctor's office or a hospital and say you have a sore throat or a kidney stone and ask what the cash price is, in most cases you will be quoted a price that is about 70% to 80% less than the insurance price (and maybe even close to 90% less as shown in the example below).

A recent (May 2018) *Wall Street Journal* article stated, "Hospitals and other providers increasingly are offering cash prices far below what they charge through insurance."

The article gave the example of a retired lawyer in Colorado who was told the knee X-ray she needed would cost her $600, out of pocket, if she used her high-deductible insurance or just $70 if she paid cash up front.

Health insurance costs and options have changed a lot lately and will probably change more by the time you read this, so rather than me trying to give you the latest information on health insurance, I'm going to give you some general information and also provide you with links showing you where you can get the absolute latest information and learn about the best options for you and your situation.

Getting healthcare when you don't live in one place can be difficult.

The major problem is finding a healthcare plan that doesn't restrict you to doctors in your network.

If you are old enough to be on Medicare, it's a lot easier because Medicare covers you in all 50 states.

One important point: If you are on Medicare, do NOT change to a Medicare Advantage plan because these have a network of doctors and you will likely be out of the network area a lot of the time. Keep your original Medicare and purchase one of the Medicare Supplement plans. These cover you in all 50 states.

If you're not old enough to be on Medicare, I suggest you hurry up and get old enough, and your insurance problems will be a lot easier.

In the meantime, there are other options.

Here are some things to consider before you sign up for a health insurance plan.

- Some insurance companies flatly don't insure RVers. Avoid these.

- Some plans require you to live in the state for at least six months out of the year. Avoid these.

- Avoid HMO plans and stick with PPO plans that have a large nationwide network of providers.

- One of the best places to get up-to-date information is on Kyle Henderson's website:

  RVerInsurance.com

  Kyle is a full-time RVer himself. Here is a link that will take you straight to the page on his website that has the latest 2018 health insurance information and options.

- **RverInsurance.com/health-insurance-2018**

In addition to the above information, here are three other websites that provide some useful information about healthcare:

- **HealthSherpa.com** — This site allows you to do comparison shopping of exchange policy plans.

- **24-7healthInsurance.com** — Coleen Elkins is one of the best in the business when it comes to health insurance information for those under 65. Check out her website or call her at 888-337-1705. She is licensed in 11 states including FL, TX, and SD.

- RVerhiexchange.com

An option to consider

If you're self-employed, not old enough for Medicare, are basically in good health, and want to stay compliant with the Affordable Care Act (ACA), here's an option you should consider. Have a plan with **Healthcare.gov**, which is commonly called the Marketplace.

I've seen payments from zero (yes, zero) up to $50 a month depending on which state you're in, what subsidy level you qualify for, and other factors. This is doable even on your $1,000 a month budget.

When you're only making $1,000 a month, your subsidy level for Affordable Care Act insurance is going to get your

out of pocket payments down to almost nothing—maybe even zero.

There are a lot of differences in the Marketplace offerings of the different states. One important fact to keep in mind is that, of the three states that most full-time RVers select as their domicile state (Texas, South Dakota, and Florida), only Florida (Florida Blue) has Marketplace plans that provide nationwide coverage.

This is important if you have health issues that require you to see your doctor frequently. You wouldn't want to have to drive from California or Georgia to South Dakota every time you needed to see a doctor.

Being able to get nationwide insurance coverage when you're not on Medicare is another reason why I recommend you seriously look at Florida as your domicile state.

One new healthcare option

If you are a member of Escapees RV club, they now offer an insurance program for RVers. You can join Escapees for $39.95 a year. This is one of the RVing clubs that I recommend you join even if you don't use their insurance program. By the way, they also offer mail forwarding services, and publish a great RVing magazine. Check them out at the link below:

Escapees.com

The Escapees RV Club has partnered with Independent Truckers Group to provide club members an alternative to traditional medical insurance. The arrangement provides exclusive insurance programs for RVers.

The program is WellMEC. It's a plan that meets the minimum coverage requirements of the Affordable Care Act, and you can pick what kind of additional coverage you want. Plans start for as little as $24.95 a month, and you can add optional dental and vision care. Check the program out at this link:

Escapees.com/benefits/escapees-healthcare-solutions

Summary of health insurance options in 2018 for pre-Medicare RVers

This is the title of a recent article posted by Nina Wheeling on her blog. Here is a link to it:

Wheelingit.us/2017/10/31

The article is up to date as of November 2017 and does an excellent job of describing and summarizing the current options for RVers who are not yet old enough to be on Medicare.

Even with insurance, getting to see a doctor may not be easy

RVerHiExchange.com - Even though you have insurance, getting an appointment to see a doctor in a city where you have never been to a doctor before can be a problem.

Here are three techniques RVers use to get to see a doctor when they're on the road.

1. Go to an emergency medical clinic.

2. Sign up with Teladoc.com. You can place a call and a board-certified doctor will call you back (usually within 10 to 15 minutes). The doctor will discuss your symptoms with you and call in a prescription to a pharmacy near you, or, if necessary, tell you if they think you need to see a specialist.

3. CVS, Walgreens, and other pharmacies now have a nurse practitioner on staff part of the time. You can walk in; they can examine you and then write a prescription for your minor health problems.

I think with all of the options provided in this section, you will be able to find a healthcare solution that will meet your needs and your budget. You will just have to do a lot of research and jump through some hoops.

How to connect to the internet

Keep in mind that, even though almost all campgrounds say they have fast, high-speed internet, you may not have a strong signal all over the campground, and during peak usage times it can get very slow.

If a high speed, reliable internet connection is important to you (and it will be if you're using it to make an income), you will probably need another option other than relying on the campground internet.

The options I use are hotspot devices. All carriers offer them, and the prices and plans are changing all the time.

Right now, I'm testing three different options. I have a Verizon JetPack, an AT&T Mobley, and a T-Mobile device. I mostly use the AT&T Mobley device because I get unlimited data for $20 a month. Unfortunately, that plan is no longer being offered, but the internet providers continue to introduce new plans all the time. Check to see what plans are available now.

Verizon has the best coverage, and T-Mobile has a plan where the data you use watching YouTube videos doesn't count against your data usage. In other words, there are advantages and disadvantages to all of your options. On top of that, the carriers are always changing their plans and prices.

When you're ready to hit the road, check out the different carriers and see which one is presently offering the best plan. Also, check their coverage maps to be sure they have good coverage in the areas where you will be traveling the most.

To find out the latest up-to-date RV internet options, I depend on Chris and Cherie. Here is a link to their website:

RVmobileinternet.com/classroom

Here is a link to a YouTube video posted in May of 2018 that summarizes the options they use to connect to the internet.

Youtube.com/watch?v=JcKyAiddQqMRvMobileInternet.com/classroom

They provide a lot of free information, and they also offer more detailed information if you become a subscriber. I subscribe to their paid subscription. To me it's well worth it to keep up with the latest internet options and changes.

How do you handle banking?

As a full-time RVer, my opinion is that you need accounts with at least two different, unrelated banks. When passwords or debit cards get lost or stolen or when there are problems of any kind with one account, having a second account could save you a lot of grief while you're getting things straightened out.

Also, when you're looking for a branch bank, if you have two banks you are a lot more likely to find one close to you.

When selecting the two banking institutions, make sure they have branches in the states you plan to travel to the most. Online banks are now a good option, too. I use Wells Fargo and Bank of America, but banks are rapidly changing the services they offer, so do your homework before selecting your two banks.

Some features you should look for when selecting banks include the ability to transfer money between accounts online, the ability to make payments online, and the ability to deposit checks by just taking a picture of the check and sending it to them. In other words, you want a bank that is very much into online banking.

You should also keep some cash hidden in your RV. There are lots of places in an RV where you could have a few hundred dollars well hidden.

What about pets and RVs?

In most campgrounds, I would say that about half of the RVs have a dog (or should I say the dog has an RV?). I don't know if any of the dogs actually drive their RV, but most of them seem to be in charge and run the show.

Seriously, pets make great companions when traveling and living the RV lifestyle. They enjoy checking out new places and seeing new things. Even cats that stay inside all of the time seem to enjoy and be intrigued by the new scenery.

All campgrounds allow pets. There are some rules that must be followed, so make sure you and your pet both read the rules. The rules are usually straightforward, common sense rules such as no barking, your dog must be on a leash, clean up after your pet, etc.

What do you do about healthcare for your pets?

First of all, be sure to keep current copies of all of your pet's vaccinations or you might end up getting duplicate and unnecessary treatments. One solution is to use a national chain of vets such as Banfield Pet Hospital. They have offices all over the country. Go to their website at **Banfield.com** and enter the zip code where you are, and you can find their closest office. Many of their offices are located inside PetSmart™ stores. They have a centralized database and your pet's records can be brought up at any of their offices. Wouldn't it be nice if doctors had the same system for us humans?

When traveling with pets, you have to pay a little bit of attention to their special needs—especially when you're away from the RV for a few hours. Make sure it doesn't get too hot or too cold and make sure they have plenty of water.

One last point about traveling with pets

Be sure to keep plenty of your pet's food on hand. You may not be able to find your normal brand everywhere (even if it's a common brand).

Changing your pet's food and then hitting the road in your RV could result in trouble for you and your pet. Don't risk it. Some people order their favorite brand of pet food on Amazon and have it shipped to wherever they are if it's a brand that's not commonly available.

Remember that pets can be expensive

If you already have a dog or a cat, I'm sure you're not going to give it away. But if you don't have a pet and you're trying to live on $1,000 a month, by all means, don't get a pet.

Some RVers tell me that they spend $100 to $200 a month on pet food. Also, vet bills can blow your budget in a heartbeat. A friend just spent $800 on a vet bill, and there was nothing wrong with her dog. It was just for his annual wellness check-up. My brother spent $1,800 on emergency surgery for his little dog because of a blocked bladder.

Having a pet may also interfere with the jobs you can accept. You might not be able to work all day if you have to get back to take your dog out during the day.

Can you RV if you have kids, and, if so, how?

Kids adjust well to life on the road. They experience so much more of life and of the real world than they ever would in a classroom or living in a typical neighborhood. With home-schooling and the internet, traveling with kids (of any age) is a very viable option.

To give you an idea of what it's like to RV with kids, here are some videos that will let you see for yourself:

• **Youtube.com/watch?v=z4QSp28ymvQ** – Nate, Marissa, and their young daughter enjoying the RVing lifestyle.

• In December of 2016, Brittany and Eric brought Caspian (or baby nomad as they sometimes call him) home from the hospital and moved him into their Class A motorhome when he was one day old. If you want to know more about how this is working out, you can follow them on their blog at **RVwanderlust.com/one-year-old-rv**

- **Youtube.com/watch?v=Youtube.com/watch?v=c2xkfk hfcEg** – Nate and Christian Axness are a young couple who travel with their two kids. I think you will find their videos interesting. Here's another one of their videos that shows them playing and hiking with their little girl. **Youtube.com/watch?v=xKLparutJhk&t=149s**

Things to consider when RVing with kids

It's important that each child has their own space. In addition to having their own bed, it's important for each child to have a special place to store personal stuff. Personal space is important. It doesn't have to be big, but it does need to be entirely the child's place.

If you're traveling with teenagers, it may be a little more difficult to make them happy about leaving their friends back home. Some things that help are involving the older kids in making the plans for where to go next. Maybe even have them go online and make reservations and map out routes and where to stop along the way.

Another thing that older kids enjoy from time to time is to have one or two of their friends come along for a week or so. If there's not enough room in the RV, pitch a tent next to it.

With the internet, Skype, Facebook, email, etc., kids can stay in touch with their friends and they'll have so many interesting adventures to share with them. Some kids even start their own blog, so their friends can keep up with them.

YouTube has lots of videos that have been posted by RVers who are living the RV lifestyle with their kids. Watch some of them and see how they do it.

Here are some more videos showing people RVing with kids that I would recommend for you to watch. You may decide to skip some of the videos that I link to, but I highly recommend that you watch this first one in the list below.

Vimeo.com/71385845

Youtube.com/watch?v=nq5s15uuG34

Youtube.com/watch?v=xjixHDkYwPw

Search YouTube for "RVing with kids" (or some similar phrase) and you will find a ton of videos about RVing with kids of all ages—from toddlers to teenagers.

Other things you have to deal with when RVing

Voting: You need to get registered to vote. You will vote in the precinct where your legal address is. In some states, you can register to vote when you get your driver's license.

When elections come up, you need to vote in both local and national elections. This will help establish the fact that you are a resident of the state you claim as your domicile. You can vote using an absentee ballot.

Family doctor and dentist: You have to think about whether you want to go back to your present family doctor and dentist for your annual check-ups. That's what I do. A lot of RVers choose to do this. They get to visit with family and friends when they're back in town. Getting back to your former home base at least once a year is something a lot of people look forward to.

You may have been spending most of your time thinking about what kind of RV to buy and how you're going to support yourself when you retire or quit your job and live in an RV, but the little things I've listed above are important, too, and have to be taken care of.

Being away from family and friends: For a lot of people this is a big deal but take it in stride and realize that you can make it to any of the family reunions or special occasions you want to. That might not have always been the situation before you started living the RVing lifestyle.

Most major family events are planned way in advance and you can plan to be there if you really want to. If you're in Arizona and the family reunion or wedding is going to be in Michigan, that could be a problem, but if you plan far enough in advance, you can make it happen.

You'll probably want to get back to your former home base from time to time anyway and visit with family and old friends. Plan and make it happen.

Bottom line: There are a lot of decisions you will need to make and things to do before you hit the road as a full-time RVer. None of these things take a lot of time or effort, but it's important that you get them done.

---------- Chapter 15 ----------

Safety and Security Concerns

"Security is mostly a superstition. It does not exist in nature, nor do the children of men as a whole experience it. Avoiding danger is no safer in the long run than outright exposure. Life is either a daring adventure or nothing."

~ Helen Keller

Safety and security concerns mainly grow out of fear of the unknown. It's human nature to fear the unknown.

If there were no unknown, there would be no adventure. How much fun would that be?

Most people who are considering the RVing lifestyle have a lot of concerns, and they worry about a lot of things.

When I think about worrying, I think of the wisdom of my grandmother. She said, "Worrying must help because most of the things I worry about never happen."

Maybe she was paraphrasing Mark Twain's quote. He said, "I've had a lot of worries in my life, most of which never happened."

I travel as a solo RVer, and I have been doing so for more than six years. It's an interesting life. I never know what I'll encounter, who I'll meet, or how long I'll stay in one place.

I guess sometimes I know how long I'll stay because sometimes I make reservations, but that's always subject to change depending on what interesting things I find to do.

RVing is exciting, challenging, and full of amazing experiences. One of the things I like about RVing is that I can change my mind and plans at any crossroad. The decisions are mine to make, and the consequences are mine to bear.

Below are what I consider to be the 11 techniques that will help you feel safe and secure as an RVer. (Note: I provided a modified version of these same 11 techniques back in Chapter 5 when discussing the topic of solo RVing. Pardon the repetition, but I think these points are important for you to keep in mind whether you're a solo RVer or traveling with someone. I also included these things in both chapters because I wanted each chapter to stand alone and completely cover the topic of the chapter.)

11 ways to help you feel safe and secure as an RVer

- **Arrive at your campground well before dark.** Don't push it close because traffic and other factors can make your trip take longer than expected. It's hard to judge the safety of a camping place after dark, and it's a lot easier to get backed in and get set up when it's daylight.

- **Meet your neighbors.** You'll feel more like one of the family after you meet a few people. You'll also feel more secure when you know some people. It's easier to meet people before dark, so that's another good reason to arrive in the daylight.

- **Carry Mace, pepper spray, a gun or whatever you feel comfortable with.** You'll probably never need or use any of these items, but they buy you peace of mind.

- **Have an extra set of keys in a metal magnetic box in a secure and out-of-the-way place outside your RV.** Nothing makes you feel more helpless than being locked out of your RV.

- **Have an extra credit card and a few hundred dollars of cash hidden inside your RV.** There are plenty of places in an RV where you can hide things that couldn't be found if someone had all day to look for them. This could really come in handy if you lose your wallet.

- **Have photocopies of the front and back of your driver's license and all of your credit cards, insurance cards, etc.** Keep a copy in your RV and also leave a copy with a friend or family member.

- **Have a GPS and know how to use it.** Also, have a good set of maps.

- **Keep your cell phone with you and keep the battery charged.** You may want to keep an extra battery. If you spend much time in areas where you don't have a good cell phone signal, consider getting a cell phone booster. Also, have one of the little 12-volt to USB adapters so you can charge your phone from your RV or vehicle.

- **Stay in one location for a week or a month or longer.** When you first arrive at a place, that's when you feel the most insecure. That's because everything is unknown to you. It's natural. The longer you stay in a place the more comfortable you will feel there. It's simple. If you stay in each place for a month at a time, you will spend most of your time feeling comfortable. If you're moving every two or three days, you will spend most of your time feeling a little uncomfortable or apprehensive. Also, you will save money by taking advantage of the lower weekly or monthly rates, you'll cut your gas expense, and you'll have time to explore the area.

- **Keep your RV well maintained.** You don't want breakdowns while you're on the road. Replace belts and hoses as soon as they start showing signs of aging. Also, be sure to check the air pressure in your tires regularly. I have an automatic system that gives me a readout on the dash of the pressure and temperature of each of my six motorhome tires, plus the two dolly tires and the two back tires of my car. In addition to the digital readout, it also sounds an alarm if the pressure of any tire gets outside the safe range I've set. This gives me peace of mind. I consider this to be the best investment I've made when it comes to gadgets or modifications to my RV.

- **The most important thing to keep in mind is to follow your instincts about safety.** If you pull into a place and your gut tells you that something doesn't seem right, your house has wheels. You can leave.

When you realize that security is not a problem for RVers, what else is there to worry about?

So, as Mark Twain said, "Throw off the bowlines. Sail away from the safe harbor. Catch the trade winds in your sails. Explore. Dream. Discover."

Bottom line: Security is one of the major concerns for many people who are thinking about living the RV lifestyle, and it's a valid concern. But it's not one that should keep you from hitting the road. Just lock your doors, use common sense, and if a place doesn't look or feel safe, leave.

Chapter 16

Make a Decision

"Most people who died yesterday had plans for today."

~ Unknown

If you want to live in an RV someday, it will never happen. I meet people all the time, and when I tell them I live full time in a motorhome, they say, "That's what I want to do one day."

They'll never do it. They're not making any serious plans to live in an RV. To them, it's just a daydream. Keep the quote at the beginning of this chapter in mind, and don't let it happen to you.

I was sitting in a marketing class at Harvard one day. The head of the marketing department was teaching the class, and the class was discussing a case.

The professor called on one guy and asked him what he would do in the situation described in the case. The student said he would go out and get more information. That was the wrong answer. Here's what the instructor said,

"Every decision you make for the rest of your life will be made with incomplete information."

He went on to say, "Make a decision, and if it turns out to be wrong, you can change it. If you don't make a decision, the problem can never be fixed."

He went on to say, "More businesses have failed because they didn't make a decision than ever failed because they made the wrong decision."

I think this same advice applies to life in general as well.

In my opinion, it's okay to be sitting in a rocking chair on the front porch of a nursing home and saying, "I thought about living full time in an RV, but after I checked into it, I decided not to do it."

I would hate to be sitting in that same rocking chair and saying, "I thought about living full time in an RV, but I never got around to making a decision about whether to do it or not."

Don't be like the second person sitting in the rocking chair. Make a decision.

Amelia Earhart said it best: "The most difficult thing is the decision to act, the rest is merely tenacity. The fears are paper tigers. You can do anything you decide to do. You can act to change and control your life."

Almost all your life, where you have lived has been dictated to a large extent by jobs or school or family or, let's face it, just plain habit.

Now you have freedom (because you declared that you have it), and this is your chance to make a decision with the main criteria being, "Where will I be the happiest and what lifestyle will I enjoy the most?"

I think not embarking on the RV lifestyle is probably the best decision for most people, but not deciding is not a good decision for anybody.

If you have the dream and the burning desire to make it happen, then make a decision and go for it. In the previous paragraph, when I said that not embarking on the RV lifestyle is probably the best decision for most people, keep in mind that you're not most people. If you were, you wouldn't be reading this book.

You're different. You have a dream. (And after reading this book you will know how to get the dime it will take to make it happen.)

Bottom line: Do a reasonable amount of research, soul-searching, and fact-finding, and then make your decision. You will never have all of the information, but remember when you're living the RV lifestyle, it's easy to change your mind, sell your RV, and live a different lifestyle.

The important things are to have a dream and to make a decision.

Chapter 17

How to Get Rid of Your Stuff

"A house is just a place to keep your stuff while you go out and get more stuff."

~ George Carlin

One of the first things you have to do after you set your departure date is get rid of your stuff.

This is one of the hardest things for a lot of people to do. Here's how to do it the easy way.

I hear people say things all the time such as, "I could never live in an RV. I have too much stuff."

They say it with the same conviction that they would say that one leg was longer than the other one. They act like they were born with all of the stuff, and there is nothing they can do about the situation.

While your house is on the market, get rid of all of your stuff that you don't need—which will be almost everything. It's easier than most people think.

If you need even more help, I wrote a book called *Tidying Up.* In addition to showing you how to tidy up once and for all and never have to do it again, the book also shows you how to decide what to get rid of.

Tidying Up: The Magic and Secrets of Decluttering Your Home and Your Life

The eBook version is available from Amazon for $3.99 at the link below:

Amazon.com/dp/B01J6EVSR4

How to get rid of your stuff

An RVing friend of mine told me about when she decided to live the RVing life. She wasn't ready to get rid of all of her stuff, so she stored everything in a barn on her parents' farm.

About a year later, the barn caught fire, and everything was destroyed. She said she should have been devastated, but she found herself feeling happy and didn't know why.

Then she realized the reason she was happy was that all of her stuff was gone, and she didn't have to feel guilty for getting rid of any of it. (The things she really wanted were already in her RV.)

It wasn't that she wanted any of the stuff; she just didn't want to get rid of it. I think that describes a lot of us.

If you say, "I choose to have all of this stuff," then you own the situation or problem. It's easier to deal with when you look at it that way.

Here are the steps to getting rid of your stuff

Your stuff can all be classified into one of four categories, A, B, C, and D.

Category A: Things you really are going to use and take with you in your RV. (You can't take all of your clothes. You have to choose.)

Category B: These are the things you can sell—your dining room table and chairs, the sofa you bought two years ago, your riding lawnmower. In fact, you can sell almost everything, and it doesn't take long to do it. Selling all of this stuff is a good way to make that "dime" bigger.

Craigslist is a great way to sell larger items that you don't want to bother to ship. If you price the items right and include pictures, they will usually sell within a week. If an item doesn't sell within a week, lower the price by at least a third and list it again.

Be sure to list a phone number where you can be reached most of the time. When someone is ready to buy something, if they can't get you on the phone, they will call another person selling essentially the same type of item you're offering. I have sold a lot of items using Craigslist. The system works great. You get a fair price and you get it sold quickly.

For smaller items that you can ship, you can use eBay. For both Craigslist and eBay, be sure to show several good quality pictures. Pictures help items sell quickly. With eBay, you can set a reserve price, or you can just auction it off and take what you get. After all, usually, whatever it sells for is what it's worth and that's what you wanted to do in the first place—sell the item for whatever it's worth.

Category C: These are the things that you put in a garage sale one Saturday and then take what doesn't sell to Goodwill. This way, at the end of the day, everything in this category is gone.

Category D: This category is for sentimental things. A few of these things you may want to put in storage—but very few. Pictures and photo albums can all be scanned and put on a thumb drive. If you don't know how to do this, there are businesses that offer this service at a reasonable price.

Most people think things on this list are the hardest to get rid of, but, in fact, these items can be the easiest to get rid of if you follow the procedure described below.

First of all, decide who you want to have each of these things when you're dead and gone. (I know you consider that to be a long way off but think about it this way anyway.) Then give the items to them now. If they won't take the things now, you know what will happen to them as soon as you're gone. They'll give them to Goodwill, sell them in a garage sale or just throw them away. If you have a few items that you want your grandchildren to have when they're grown, you can put these items in storage if you can't convince their parents to keep the items for them.

I know it's hard to accept the fact that a lot of things you cherish will not even be considered worth keeping by other people when you're gone. That's just a fact. Don't blame your relatives. It's not their responsibility or duty to like or value the same things you do.

A lot of the things you will be giving people will be things they will love and really enjoy having. By giving them the items now, you'll get to see them enjoy the things and you'll know the items went to the people you wanted to have them.

By all means, don't just put things in storage—at least, not more than what will fit in the smallest storage unit they make.

If you do put things in a storage unit, consider getting rid of even those things a year from now. Some people have found it easier to get rid of sentimental things in a two-step process like this, but don't let it drag out for years and still have your belongings in storage.

In other words, put those things you think you just can't part with in storage for one year. At the end of a year, decide if your future is full-time RVing. If so, give everything that's in storage that you're not actually going to use to your relatives. If they don't want it, sell it. If it doesn't sell, give it to Goodwill or throw it away.

It will feel like a tremendous burden is lifted from your shoulders when you have gotten rid of all of the stuff you don't really need.

There is some wiggle room

Now that I've convinced you to get rid of most of your stuff and shown you how to do it, let me back up and tell you that you do have a little bit of wiggle room. Many RVers get a small storage unit and they keep a few things they're not ready to get rid of yet.

But in a year or so, you should get rid of the things in the storage unit.

I know one couple who took a picture of their empty storage unit and then threw a party and invited their friends to help them celebrate the big occasion. It was a fun time.

Plan your party now to celebrate your freedom from STUFF!

One final point: Don't go through your stuff and decide what to throw away. Go through it and decide what to keep. The best way to decide what to keep is to ask yourself, "Does this really bring me joy?" If you're truthful with yourself, you'll decide that most items don't really bring you any joy, so don't keep them. It's that simple.

Bottom line: You have all of this stuff because you chose to have it. Therefore, you can choose to get rid of it. You may not believe it now, but it's such a big relief when you get rid of all of the stuff you've been hanging on to for years.

━━━━━ **Chapter 18** ━━━━━

Make it Happen

"Don't wait. The time will never be just right."

~ Napoleon Hill

We are all procrastinators by nature and by habit. We've been making decisions and then putting off taking action all our lives. In a lot of cases, we even put off making decisions. It's just human nature.

Some people make things happen, some people watch things happen, and some people wonder what happened. To live the RVing life, you have to be a person who makes things happen.

Look at it this way, if three birds were sitting on a fence and one decided to fly away, how many would be left? If birds are anything like us humans, there would probably still be three birds on the fence. Just because one bird decided to fly away doesn't mean he actually did it. We decide to do things all the time and then never do them.

Hopefully, you have already done the two hard things. You've made the decision, and you've set the departure date.

Now you have to **make things happen**.

You can't say, "I'm going to hit the road and live in an RV when I get everything taken care of or when (fill in the blank)." If that's your approach, it will never happen.

There are a lot of steps involved

To make your dream of living life as a full-time RVer come true, there are a lot of things that have to be done.

Everything has to fall (or be pushed) into place to make your RVing lifestyle a reality.

There are so many things you have to do or make decisions about that it's hard to even know where to start. It can seem overwhelming.

Of course, one of the first things you have to make a decision about (and then take action on) is what to do with your house.

If you're living in a rented apartment or condo, things are a lot simpler. The day your lease expires could be the day you hit the road.

Selling your house

If you own a house, things can get complicated. One of the first things you need to do is take steps to get your house sold or rented. This will be one of your biggest obstacles. Take steps to solve this problem as soon as you make your decision to live in an RV.

Call a real estate agent and get your house on the market to sell or rent. Tell your real estate agent that you want to set a price that will make your house sell in a reasonable amount of time. Then listen to what she tells you.

Don't sit around idle and wait for the house to sell. Since you've already set a date when you're going to hit the road, get busy taking care of the other things that must be done.

A word about selling your house. I know people who have had their houses on the market for two or three years and they still haven't sold them. A lot of people have an unrealistic expectation about what their houses are worth. Don't fall into this trap. It's worth what it will sell for now.

The main reason a house doesn't sell is that the owner has set an unrealistic price. Set your price at a fair market value (or maybe a little less), and your house will sell. Right now, houses are selling fast, so if you have set a fair price for your house, it will sell.

Put your house on the market, set a fair price, and if it doesn't sell within a reasonable amount of time, lower the price and keep doing this until it sells or until you decide to keep the house and rent it out. At that point, get it rented.

One other thing to be prepared for is that your house might sell within a few days. I was talking to a couple at an RV park recently, and they said they had a contract on their house three days after they put it on the market. They had to get rid of everything and vacate the house in 30 days. My brother had a full-price contract on his house three hours after he put it on the market.

Another friend sold her house for the full asking price about two weeks after it was listed. Houses are selling fast now and usually at or near the asking price.

Normally, getting a contract on your house is a good thing, but if you're not ready for it to sell, you might have to get ready pretty quickly.

A few years ago, my neighbor had her place on the market for over a year and then finally sold it for less than she had turned down a month after it was listed. Your house is worth what it will sell for now.

My mother and father sold their house (and a lot of the stuff inside it) at an auction. Maybe you're not that brave, but a good auction company will get you a fair price for your house. I'm not recommending that you have an auction to sell your house, but if all else fails, it's an option.

If you don't have a deadline, you will never get to the end of your to-do list.

Not everything has to be done before you hit the road

You are not like Lewis and Clark heading off into the wilderness for two years. You can do things while you're on the road.

For example, you want to get your banking set up with two banks that have branches nationwide. It would be nice if this could be taken care of before you left, but you could do it while you're on the road.

You may want a better (or a lower priced) car to tow behind your motorhome or a different truck to tow your camper. You can sell your present car or truck and then buy something else while you're on the road.

Of course, if you're going to get a fifth-wheel or a camper, one of the first things you will need to do (after you decide what kind and size of camper you want) is buy a truck. You can't bring a camper home until you have a truck to pull it with.

Concentrate on taking care of the things that absolutely must be taken care of before you leave. Remember, you have a departure date. If you didn't get your riding lawn mower sold, give it to somebody. You'll be surprised how fast things happen when you really do have a firm departure date.

You always have the option of renting a storage unit for those items you're not ready to part with.

The next step is to start making things fall into place

After you set a date, take action. As I said before, the hardest thing for most people to do is to get rid of most of their "stuff," so start this process early—like now.

Adopt Larry the Cable Guy's motto of "Git-R-Done." Another saying I like is, "Done trumps everything."

Not everything on your list will get done. In fact, not everything has to be done before you leave.

It's more important that you get things done than it is to get them done perfectly

You've been told all your life to do your best, but not everything needs your best effort.

For example, consider the situation where you're baking cupcakes and they crumble when you take them out of the pan. If you're baking them for the Cub Scouts, put more icing on the cupcakes and serve them.

On the other hand, if you're baking cupcakes for the bridge club, maybe you better start over and bake another batch.

My grandmother would roll over in her grave if she heard me say this, but. . .

If something only halfway needs doing, only halfway do it

That's the way it is with getting ready to live the RV lifestyle. Not every step in the process requires your best effort.

It's more important that you get rid of your stuff than it is to get the very best price possible for each item. Keep the big picture in mind and make sure you're making progress (and getting things done on schedule).

Once you've made the decision to quit your job and live in an RV, don't waste time second-guessing yourself.

Six months or a year down the road you can re-evaluate the situation and if living as a full-time RVer isn't making you happy, you can sell your RV, buy a boat, move to a different country, or buy or rent a house or condo, and live wherever you wish. You're not locked into your RVing decision permanently.

People ask me how long I am going to continue living full time in a motorhome. My answer is simple, "Until it's no longer fun."

Back to reality

You made your decision before you got to this chapter. Don't keep rethinking your decision. This chapter gave you an overview of how to make it happen; now it's your job to follow through, implement the steps outlined, and really make it happen. Get busy.

Bottom line: As you get closer to your departure date, it will start to feel like crunch time. There will be a ton of things that will still need to be done and not much time to do them. Don't give in to changing your departure day. If you change it once, you'll change it again and again, and the process could drag on forever.

You've handled crunch time and deadlines all your life, you can handle one more. This one is important. Make it happen. After all, you have a dream.

Chapter 19

Summing It All Up

"When in doubt, choose change."

~ Lily Leung

Hopefully, now that you've read this book, you have your dream clearly defined, you know what you want to do, and you know how to make it happen.

My guess is that you want to live in an RV, hit the road, and never look back.

If that doesn't describe you, then you probably stopped reading this book way before you got to this point.

I've shown you how to live on a dime (or at least on a lot less than you're spending now), and I've even shown you ways to make an extra dime or two to make life on the road even more enjoyable.

You have your dime and your dream, and you're ready to get started

But I want to caution you (as I said in Chapter 2), RVing is not all rainbows, sunsets, and margaritas. I get carried away sometimes when I'm talking about the RVing lifestyle, and I'm sure I make it sound more glamorous than it is.

I think I've talked a lot more about the pros than I have the cons. This implies that living the RV lifestyle would be the best choice for almost everyone.

In reality, I think just the opposite is true. When I think of all of the people I know, relatives, close friends, and general acquaintances, in almost every case, after thinking about it, I realize that most of them would not really enjoy this lifestyle.

Therefore, I have concluded that this is not the lifestyle for most people. It's only for people who love adventure and are not afraid of change or the unknowns. My guess is that describes you.

The people I meet in the RV parks seem happy with their lifestyle, and it's easy to think that everyone would love this lifestyle. The people who probably wouldn't like it and the people who have tried it and know they don't like it are not in the RV parks, so I don't get to talk to them.

There will be problems when you're RVing, and things will break. Dealing with all of the things that break on an RV could drive some people batty, but if you can go with the flow and deal with problems and make adjustments, the RV lifestyle might work for you. My thoughts are that if you're not sure by now that you want to live the RVing lifestyle, it's probably not the lifestyle for you.

Millions of people dream of being an RVer, but they never do it. It's not that they decide not to do it; most of them just never get around to making the decision either way.

You can live in an RV and have everything you want

RVers are happy with less because they have everything they want. Anybody who lives on less because they choose to already has everything they want. The secret is to change your wants. You no longer need to keep up with the Joneses to be happy.

I don't want to make the RVing lifestyle sound like the perfect lifestyle. Describe things the right way and you could make almost anything sound like fun. Remember,

Tom Sawyer convinced his friends that whitewashing a fence was fun.

A final thought about the RVing lifestyle

Making this big a change in your life will result in an upheaval of everything you know. There will be risks, and they will result in stress. Accept this as normal, deal with the stress, and go on with your life.

As of now, RVing is in your blood. I think your decision has already been made, so set a date and make it happen. The timing will never be perfect, so make it happen now, and start enjoying your new lifestyle.

Hit the road and soak in whatever slice of nature you can. Breathe in deeply and experience the calm of the wilderness. Feel renewed and live a life with no stress. What are you waiting for?

Steve Jobs said,

"I want to put a ding in the universe."

I think you're ready to put your ding in the universe. Go for it.

Bottom line: Remember this:

"People don't take trips, trips take people."

                                            ~ John Steinbeck

If you're ready for a trip to take you, it's time to make it happen. Set your departure date, and then hit the road.

If you have questions for me, feel free to email me at

Jminchey@gmail.com

I would love to hear from you.

Chapter 20

Other Resources

"If you can't explain it to a six-year-old, you don't understand it yourself."

~ Albert Einstein

This chapter contains information on resources that I think you will find helpful. Many of these links and resources have been pointed out previously in different parts of the book, but I'm including them here so you will have what I consider to be the most useful references all in one place.

I have placed the links in categories. Some of the links could fit into more than one category, but I tried to put them in the category they best fit in. You will find a few of the links listed in more than one category. I did this in order to make the categories more comprehensive.

Blogs I follow

LessJunkMoreJourney.com – Nathan and Marissa publish one of my favorite blogs.

They also post new YouTube videos five days a week. Subscribe to their YouTube Channel to be notified when new videos are posted.

They are a young couple who sold everything and now live full time in an RV with their toddler.

Technomadia.com – Cherie and Chris have been full-time RVing for over 10 years. They say a technomadia is a technology-enabled nomad. That's where the name of their website came from. They travel in a very fancy converted bus that they have geeked-out. Their site is a wealth of information for all aspects of RVing and especially for anything to do with technology or traveling. They have written a great book, *The Mobile Internet Handbook*, which is the Bible when it comes to getting connected to the Internet while on the road. They update the book often. You can find this book (and their other books and apps) on their website and on Amazon. (Note: They now live part of the year in their motorhome and part of the year on their boat.)

Wheelingit.us – Nina and Paul Wheeling travel in a 40-foot Class A motorhome. Nina writes one of the most information-rich blogs on the Internet. They do a lot of boondocking and she writes some wonderful blog posts on boondocking as well as traveling and other RVing subjects. (Update: As of 2018 they have now sold their motorhome and moved to France, but she still writes an interesting blog about traveling.) Will they soon be RVing in France?

GoneWithTheWynns.net – Nikki and Jason Wynn sold everything, bought an RV and off they went to discover the world—at least the part they could get to in their motorhome. They provide a lot of great articles and entertaining, high-quality videos that cover their travels, equipment, and all aspects of RVing.

(Update: Back in October, 2017, they sold their motorhome and bought a catamaran sailboat and are living full time on their sailboat, sailing around the Caribbean.) They are adding a lot of articles and videos now about sailing, but the vast archives of RVing articles and videos on their website are well worth looking at. Reading their blog is fun, enjoyable, and informative. You'll love it.

Interstellarorchard.com – Becky Schade is in her mid-30s, college educated, and a single, female RVer who has been living full time in her 17-foot Casita camper for almost five years. She lives on a very tight budget and pays for her lifestyle by doing workamping at Amazon, working at national parks, and sometimes she does other gigs. She also supplements her income by writing. Her book, *Solo Full-time RVing on a Budget – Go Small, Go Now,* is a great book if you're on a tight budget and looking to get started RVing. You can find the book on her website and on Amazon. When you visit her website, be sure to click on the link to *"Start here"* in the top navigation bar. It is useful stuff. She has a new book out now, *The Little Guide to Dreaming BIG.*

CheapRVLiving.com – Bob Wells has been living in a van for 15 years. He boondocks most of the time and lives mainly off of his Social Security income plus income from writing, and occasionally he does some workamping jobs as a camp host. In addition to explaining how he lives, he also writes some great blog posts (that include wonderful pictures) about his travels and where he's camping. He also posts some interesting videos on his YouTube channel. He also posts videos where he interviews other full-time RVers.

Blog.Feedspot.com/rv_blogs – You can learn a lot from blogs and if you want to follow even more blogs than the ones I've listed here, this link will take you to a list of what is called the "**Top 100 RV Blogs**."

It also provides a brief description of each one. I don't follow all 100 of these blogs - if I did I wouldn't have time to do anything else - but take a look at the list and see if any of them look interesting to you. My guess is you'll find some you like.

RV forums

Reading forums is a great way to learn about RVing. You can see what questions other RVers are asking (and see the answers being posted by fellow RVers). You can also get answers to your own questions. Here are the three popular RV forums I follow almost every day.

RV.net/forum – Note that this website has a dot-**net** and not a dot-**com** suffix. The discussion group is broken into several categories—Class A, Fifth-wheels, Workamping, etc. Check out the different discussion groups and you will learn a lot. I check into these forums almost daily.

RV-dreams.ActiveBoard.com – This is an active discussion forum with the discussions sorted by topics. Check out the *Community Chat* section, the *Buying an RV*, and the *RV Maintenance* sections, or others that look interesting to you.

iRV2.com/forumsiRV2.com/forums – This is another active RVing forum that I check frequently.

Other RVing Forums – In addition to the popular forums listed above, there are forums for just about every brand and type of RV (Roadtrek, Airstream, National, Casita, Fleetwood, Forest River, Tiffin, etc.). Search Google and find the forum for your rig. It will be a great place to get answers to the many questions you will have about your RV. For example, "Where is the fuse for the water pump?" Your manual may not tell you, but someone on the forum for your type of RV will know and tell you almost immediately.

Finding campgrounds

Sometimes I pay the full price for a campsite, but most of the time I get discounts of 50% or more. There are two main ways I get the 50% discounts. First, I can almost always get discounts of 50% or more by booking a campsite for a month at a time. That's what I usually do. The second way I get the 50% discounts is by using one of the websites or apps below:

PassportAmerica.com – Membership is $44 a year and you get a 50% discount at 2,000 campgrounds all around the country. Stay two or three nights and you've paid for your whole year's membership. I consider being a member of

Passport America one of the best investments in the RV world.

AllStays.com – This site has a lot of campground and travel information. You can also get their information as an app for your iPhone, iPad, iPod or Android device at **AllStays.com/apps.**

Rvparking.comRVparking.com – This site has reviews and recommendations for 19,000 campgrounds. One thing I like about this site is that you get to see why people like or dislike a particular campground.

OvernightRVparking.com – Membership is $24.95 a year. They have the web's largest database of free RV parking locations in the US and Canada. Their database contains 13,605 RV Parking and No Parking locations in the USA and Canada. Search by your current location, city and state, or province or zip code. Download PDF files by state or province.

UltimateCampgrounds.com – This site provides comprehensive information on over 31,000 public campgrounds of all types in the US and Canada. They also have an app.

America the Beautiful Senior Pass – If you're 62 or older and are a US citizen, you can purchase the *America the Beautiful National Parks and Federal Recreational Lands Pass.* It's also called the *Senior Pass.* It's $80 for a lifetime membership if you buy it in person or $90 if you want to receive it by mail. It allows you free admission and discount camping (which is usually a 50% discount).

If you're not 62, you can get the Annual Pass with the same benefits.

You can get either one of the passes by mail by going to this website:

store.usgs.gov/pass/senior.html

To find locations where you can get the pass in person, go to:

store.usgs.gov/pass/PassIssuanceList.pdf

I recently camped at Curtis Creek campground in the Pisgah National Forest in North Carolina. There were 14 campsites there and only two of them were occupied. With the pass the cost was only $2.50 a night to camp and enjoy some of the most beautiful views in the North Carolina Mountains. You have to go about three miles up the mountain on a gravel road, but there is no problem getting a Class A motorhome to the campground.

FreeCampsites.net – This is a free website that allows you to search for free camping places. You can enter a city and state or a zip code and see a map showing free camping places. In most cases, there is information about each site in addition to its location.

HarvestHosts.com – This is a great resource for finding farms and wineries all over the country where you can camp overnight for free. Staying overnight at a winery or farm is a fun experience. Membership is $44 a year. I find it well worth the membership fee. Harvest Hosts provides you the opportunity to travel to new areas, have unique experiences and enjoy purchasing locally grown and produced products. (You are expected to buy a bottle or two of wine or some fruits or vegetables.)

CasinoCamper.net – Most casinos will allow you to camp overnight and many of them will even give you some free chips (they want to get you inside, so you will start gambling). If your luck is like mine, this option might end up costing you more than just paying to camp at an RV park.

Walmart – Most people don't think of Walmart as an RV park, but most Walmart stores allow RVers free overnight parking. In April (when the snowbirds were all leaving Florida and heading north), I spent the night in a Walmart parking lot and there were about 40 other RVs there. They started coming in about 5:00 p.m., and most of them were gone by 8:00 the next morning. Be sure to call or check with the manager to get permission. In some locations, city or county ordinances make it illegal to park overnight in the Walmart parking lots.

BoondockersWelcome.com – This website lists hundreds of places where you can boondock free of charge. You will generally be camping in other RVers' driveways. It's $24.95 a year if you will only be a guest and $19.95 if you have a place and agree to also let RVers camp free in your driveway.

When you agree to be a host and let people boondock in your driveway, they don't just show up. They contact you and get permission. You only let people boondock at your place when it's convenient for you. If you're going to be out of town or having company, you probably don't want boondockers during that time.

I haven't used this website yet, but everyone I've talked to who has used it said they had a wonderful experience when they did. The hosts are friendly, gracious, and happy to have you. They like to have fellow RVers to talk to and visit with.

RVing videos I like

Search YouTube for the word "RV" and you will find five million videos. Some are extremely useful and informative; some contain bad and untrue information. Some are interesting and entertaining, and some are just plain boring.

I haven't watched all five million of the videos, but I have watched a lot of them (and I do mean a lot). Below are some of the ones I consider to be worth your time to watch. Turn off the TV and spend an hour or so watching these videos, and you will be entertained and informed.

Many of the videos I have linked to here have been linked to previously in other chapters. I'm providing the links here, so you will have what I consider to be the most important RV videos in one place.

Note #1. I have watched a lot of YouTube videos, and one thing I've found is that on most videos I can speed them up to 1.5x the speed and still understand what's being said. This allows me to watch more videos in the time I've set aside to watch YouTube videos. To do this, click on the little gear symbol in the bottom right corner of the video and then click on "Speed." A pop-up menu will appear. Click on 1.5 and see how you like it.

Note #2. When you're watching these videos, you will see other videos on the page by the same people or about the same topic. Check out some of these. Watching YouTube videos about RVing is an entertaining way to quickly learn a lot about RVs and the RVing lifestyle.

Note #3. Most of these videos have been linked to previously in the book. I'm including them here, so you'll have them all in one place.

Now I'll get on with the list of videos:

Vimeo.com/71385845 – I love this 7-minute video. It's about a young couple and their full-time RVing adventure traveling with a small child. Take a look at it. I think you'll like it.

YouTube.com/watch?v=NGxmSGf2Kr8– This 14-minute video shows 17 full-time RVers as they describe how they make a living while living the RVing lifestyle. If you're looking to make some extra money while you enjoy RVing, maybe you can get some ideas from these RVers.

YouTube.com/watch?v=g0UJAMNXJbk – This 8-minute video is an interview with a retired couple describing their life on the road and how and why they decided to make the transition to the full-time RVing lifestyle.

YouTube.com/watch?v=jAhBnq2pLNk – This is another 8-minute video interview with a retired couple.

YouTube.com/watch?v=ebbo800_Rg0 – This 11-minute video interview is with a young, single, female RVer. If you're thinking about being a solo RVer, I think you will find her story interesting. By the way, she has now been on the road for 4+ years and still loves the lifestyle.

YouTube.com/watch?v=E6_AYrdfDS0 – Nathan and Marissa have had four RVs in three years, and in this video, they talk about what they wish they had known before they started their RVing life. (Note: Since this video was posted, they have changed from a Class A motorhome to an Airstream travel trailer.)

YouTube.com/results?search_query=rvgeeks – This is a link to a list of how-to RV videos by RV Geeks. You will find a lot of useful information in these videos.

YouTube.com/watch?v=7AR4uOmGfxc – This is a link to one of Kyle and Olivia's *Drivin' and Vivin'* Q&A videos. They are a young couple living full time in their tiny camper. Check out several of their videos. I think you will find them interesting. They are now in the process of renovating an Airstream camper.

YouTube.com/watch?v=BsEs-CLBbaU&t=98s – Marc and Tricia travel with their three kids and a golden retriever. They have posted several fun, interesting, and informative RVing videos.

YouTube.com/watch?v=c2xkfkhfcEg – Nate and Christian Axness are a young couple who travel with their two kids. I think you will find their videos interesting.

TechNomadia.com/ramblings – If you like the interview style of videos, this link will take you to dozens of these videos produced by Chris and Cherie at **Technomadia.com.**

YouTube.com/watch?v=bkiK5ZUgLT8– Here is a short 40-second video by Pippi Peterson. She is a young, single female who lives and travels full time in her 1992 Class A motorhome. She posts a new video every week about her RV life on the road, and, believe it or not, about RV maintenance and modifications that she does herself. She has now sold her Class A motorhome and is RVing in a fifth-wheel.

YouTube.com/watch?v=xsiLyjgQyzE – In 2012 Lidia bought a 28-foot Class C motorhome and hit the road with her 10-year-old son. She later changed to a 28-foot travel trailer and then a truck camper. This video explains why she likes the truck camper the best.

YouTube.com/watch?v=xoy3vNUjLOU – Carolyn is a 50-year-old, single woman who quit her high-paying corporate job and now lives full time in her 29-foot Class C motorhome. In this video she explains why she decided to change her lifestyle.

RVing books I like

With most eBooks priced at $2.99 to $3.99, you can get a lot of RVing information for very little money. Here are some of my favorite RVing books.

(Note: Many of these books have been linked to in previous chapters.)

Buying a Used Motorhome – How to get the most for your money and not get burned by Bill Myers.

Don't even think about buying a motorhome without reading this book. The information in this book saved me thousands of dollars. And, more importantly, it helped me pick the right motorhome for my needs and budget.

The book is about buying a used motorhome, but a lot of the information would also be useful and helpful if you were considering buying a travel trailer or fifth-wheel camper. You can find the book on Amazon at this link:

Amazon.com/dp/B007OV4TBY

Solo Full-time RVing on a Budget – Go Small, Go Now by Becky Schade. You can find the book on Amazon at this link:

Amazon.com/dp/B00W30OFCE

Or you can find it on her website at
InterstellarOrchard.com

She has another book, *The Little Guide to Dreaming BIG*. You can find it at this link:

Amazon.com/dp/B01HREJMZK

Road Cash – This book shows you dozens of step-by-step ways RVers are making money while living on the road. I just finished reading it and it's excellent. I have already been using some of the techniques discussed, and they work just as described. There are many other location-independent, income-producing methods described that

I'm eager to implement. Here's a link to the book on Amazon:

Amazon.com/dp/B0721832MD

The Mobile Internet Handbook - For US Based RVers, Cruisers & Nomads (2018 version) – This comprehensive guide to mobile internet options for US-based RVers was written by full-time RVing technomads Chris and Cherie. You can get the book on Amazon at this link:

Amazon.com/dp/B079JW8W69

Convert Your Minivan into a Mini RV Camper by William H. Myers. For $200 to $300 and a minivan, you can have an RV that you can comfortably live in. You can find the book on Amazon at this link:

Amazon.com/dp/1530265126

How to Live in a Car, Van, or RV: And Get Out of Debt, Travel, and Find True Freedom by Bob Wells. You can find the book on Amazon at this link:

Amazon.com/dp/1479215889

RV Basic Training Manual – Motorhome Driving Course. Learn what every commercial driver MUST know, and every RV driver SHOULD know. The book is a little pricey at $30 but well worth it. It's a 46-page manual with a lot of pictures and drawings, so it's easy to read. You can order it at this website:

RvBasicTraining.com/buy-manual.html

Get What's Yours – The secrets to Maxing Out Your Social Security by Laurence J. Kotlikoff and Philip Moeller. The book has been revised to cover the new 2016 laws. You can get the book from Amazon at:

Amazon.com/dp/B00LD1OPP6

This is the tenth book I've written about the different aspects of RVing. You can find a complete list of my RVing books on the right panel of my website at **LifeRV.com** or look at the last two pages of this book for a list. They are all available on Amazon.

RVing novels

If you're looking for some great novels with plots built around RVing, I would recommend the Mango Bob series. The series includes *Mango Bob, Mango Lucky, Mango Bay, Mango Glades, Mango Key, Mango Blues, and Mango Digger.*

They all revolve around a 35-year-old single guy and his adventures as he lives and travels around Florida in his motorhome. I have read all of the books in this series and I love them. I think my favorite is the last one, *Mango Digger.* I really liked *Mango Glades* too. It's hard to pick a favorite. I liked them all.

You can find them on Amazon at this link:

Amazon.com/dp/1889562033

RVing groups

Escapees.com – I recommend joining this group. It's $39.95 a year and you also get membership in the new **Xscapers.com** group (which is for younger RVers) at no extra charge. With your membership you will receive their printed magazine every other month. I consider this the most useful RVing magazine in the industry. They also offer discounts on insurance, camping, and a lot of other things I spend money on. Take a look at their website and see if you think what they offer would be useful to you.

RVillage.com – This is a free website and it's a great way to keep up with where your RVing friends are and let them know where you are.

FMCA.com – The Family Motor Coach Association is a popular group with RVers. The organization has been around for a long time. Take a look at their website and the benefits they offer. The cost is $50 for the first year and $40 for renewals. One of the things they offer is a program for getting great discounts on Michelin tires. They also host awesome RVing rallies. There were over 3,000 RVs at one of their recent rallies.

Getting healthcare on the road is changing

Important note: How the government will be changing healthcare options is totally unknown right now. I'm sure there will be changes in 2019, so be sure to check the six websites listed below to get the latest information.

- RverInsurance.com

- RverHIExchange.com

- HealthSherpa.com

- RVerInsurance.com

- RverHIExchange.comHealthSherpa.com

- Teladoc.comTeladoc.com – 24/7 access to a doctor, by phone

- 24-7HealthInsurance.com

- Wheelingit.us/2017/10/31 – This is a comprehensive article that does a great job of describing and summarizing the current options for RVers who are not yet old enough to be on Medicare. It is up to date as of November 2017. Be sure to check it out.

How to find work as an RVer

If you're RVing full time or thinking about it and want to do some part-time work while you're RVing, the websites below will be useful to you.

CoolWorks.com – This is a free site.

CoolWorks.com/jobs-with-rv-spaces – This link goes directly to a page on the above website that probably has what you're looking for.

Workamper.com – This is a subscription website. The cost is $27 a year.

Work-for-Rvers-and-Campers.com

Apps

AllStays.com/apps/camprv.htm –This is the app I use the most. With this app I can find reviews of almost 30,000 campgrounds, find locations of dump stations, find overhead clearances, and even find grades on steep mountain roads. It costs $9.99 to download the app to your iPhone or Android device.

Google Maps – In my opinion Google Maps is more accurate than Apple Maps, and it's free.

RVParking.com – This app contains almost a quarter of a million reviews of 20,000 campgrounds. The price is right for this app—it's free.

US Public Lands: You can find information about public lands with this app:

TwoStepsBeyond.com/apps/USPublicLands

About 47% of the land in the western part of the US is owned by the government. If you've ever wanted to know where to camp free on government land, you'll love this app. This app shows BLM, Forest Service, NPS, and public land boundary maps. You can download the app from Google Play or iTunes.

Reserve.WanderingLabs.com – When you check for availability at a campground and there's no campsite available on the dates you want to camp, instead of checking back every few days, let this app do it for you. Instead of checking back every few days, it will check every few minutes and send you an email as soon as a space becomes available.

The app is free, but if you want to make a small donation, you can get the version that checks constantly instead of every few minutes.

Waze.com – Your smartphone can be a reasonable substitute for an RVer specific GPS. By RVer specific GPS, I mean one that gives you information about bridge clearances, grades, dump stations, etc.

Having a hands-free phone holder in the RV is key for this.

This app also has real-time info on road conditions, traffic backups, and speed traps. It's called Waze. You can download it at **Waze.com**. I really like it. The price is right too—it's free.

Copilotgps.com/en-us/rv-navigation – Don't pay $300 to $500 for a GPS device with all of the information RVers need. You can get this app that will turn your phone into GPS especially for RVs for $39.99.

GasBuddy.com – Find the lowest price on gas wherever you are, and it's free.

Snapseed – Easy and simple basic photo editing while you travel. You can download it on your computer or download the app for your phone.

Other websites

Spend an evening or two reading the articles and watching the videos you'll find on the websites listed below and you'll know more about RVing than most of the RVers out there. Best of all, I think you'll find the way the information is presented in these videos, blogs, and articles to be enjoyable and entertaining.

I check these websites for new information at least once a week. Most of them have a way to sign up and get an email message when new information is posted.

Technomadia.com – Chris and Cherie have been full-time RVers for more than 10 years. They share a lot of useful information on their site. They have a big converted bus that they have done wonders with and made it fancy and functional. Spend some time on their website, and you will soon know a lot more than most long-time RVers. New articles are posted every week, and there are a lot of video interviews on this site that you will find interesting. Note: They now spend half of their time living and traveling on their boat.

RV-Dreams.com – Howard and Linda have a website that's full of information and personal experiences. Turn the TV off and spend a night reading and absorbing the wealth of information they have to offer. There is also a lively discussion forum on the site. You can find a link to their discussion forum in the left nav panel on their site. Howard quit being an attorney several years ago and they hit the road and became full-time RVers.

InterstellarOrchard.com – Becky Schade is a 34-year-old, college educated, single female living full time in her RV. She does workamping and writing to fund her travels. On her site, you can read her articles, and you can learn more about what she does and her solo RVing lifestyle. She posts a couple of new articles every week and I think you will find them enlightening and interesting. Some of her articles are about her travels, and some are about what she does, what she thinks, and her life in general on the road as a full-time single, female RVer.

CheapRvLiving.com – Bob Wells has a ton of information on his website about living in a van. He has lived in it full time and traveled for many years. He lives mostly on his Social Security. Check out his website and see how he does it.

Motorhome.com/download-dinghy-guides – Some cars can be towed with all four wheels down and some require that you use a dolly. At this site, for $1.99, they offer a downloadable guide. They have a different guide for each model year. If you already own a car that you're considering towing, be sure to check your car's owner's manual to see if it can be towed with all four wheels down.

PplMotorhomes.com/sold/soldmenu.htm – This site tells you what RVs have recently sold for. The people at PPL Motorhomes sell about 4,000 motorhomes a year, and they show you what each one actually sold for. They also always have a huge inventory of used RVs for sale. Most of them are on consignment.

RVSchool.com – This is a great RV driving school. They teach you to drive in your own motorhome. Take a look at their schedule and see if they're going to be offering training at a rally near you. They offer discounts at most RV rallies.

Use **Yelp.com** to find recommended local services—dentists, restaurants, auto repair shops, computer repair shops, etc.

There are thousands of good sources of information on the internet (and, of course, thousands of sites with information that's not so useful). The links I have provided in this chapter are to the RVing resources (books, forums, videos, apps, and websites) that I use the most and the ones I think provide really useful and trusted information. I highly recommend you take a look at all of the resources I have linked to in this chapter and throughout the book.

If you have questions for me, feel free to email me at **Jminchey@gmail.com** or go to my website at **RVLife.com** to learn more about the RV lifestyle and adventure. On the website, you can post your questions in the discussion forum and you will get answers from me and other RVers.

Whether you enjoy the RVing adventure or whether you find it frustrating will be determined a lot by your attitude. Spend some time watching the videos and reading the blogs I've linked to in this chapter, and I think when you realize how much fun other RVers are having and how much they are enjoying the adventure, it will help you realize how wonderful this lifestyle can be.

Bottom Line: If you're considering becoming an RVer, realize that there is a lot to learn in order to safely and economically enjoy the RV lifestyle. Check out the links in this chapter, and you will be well on your way to becoming an informed and experienced RVer.

In order to live the RV lifestyle on a dime and a dream, you must be knowledgeable and fully informed about a lot of aspects of RVing. The information in this book (including the information at the links provided) will arm you with the information you need.

Did You Like This Book?

If you liked this book, I need your help.

I would appreciate it if you would take a minute and leave a review on Amazon. (You really can do it in only one minute.)

Writing a review is not like writing a high school book report. All you need to do is write a sentence or two saying that you liked the book.

Thank you,

Jerry Minchey

On the following pages are some of my other RVing books that you might find interesting and entertaining.

(You can find them on Amazon.)

Other books by the author available on Amazon

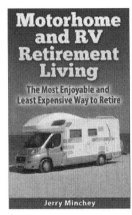
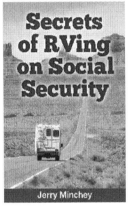

More books by the author available on Amazon

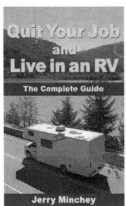

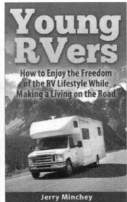

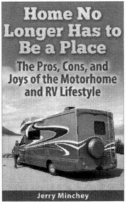

Made in the USA
Middletown, DE
28 May 2020

96212149R00121